Deep Reflection

ADVANCING THE MEDICI FUSION

201 VISUAL EXPLORATIONS OF CROSS-BORDER THINKING

Leo Yuan, Ph.D.

More Than 40 Years of Experience
Teaching Creative Thinking

Advancing the Medici Fusion

Copyright © Leo Yuan 2024
All rights reserved. No part of this publication may be reproduced, stored in a retrieval system, or transmitted in any form or by any means, mechanical, photocopying, recording or otherwise, without prior permission in writing of the author.
ISBN: 978-1-7351164-6-4

leoyuan@ms4.hinet.net

LEO YUAN, PH.D.

Table of Contents

The Unique Arrangement of Epiphanies in This Book. 3
The Basic Principles of Cross-Border Thinking............ 8
Invention Principles Topic 32
Invention Principles Cross-Border Association 73
Verb Thinking Cross-Border Association 131
Set Theme Cross-Border Association 178

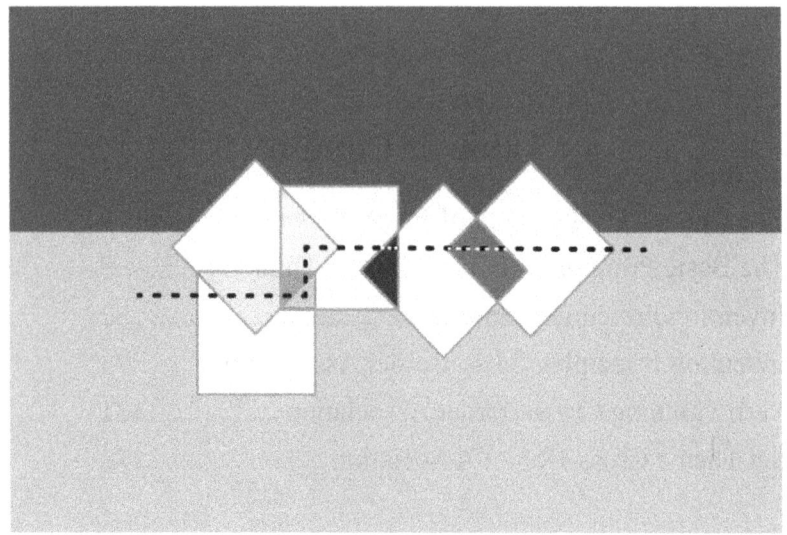

The Unique Arrangement of Epiphanies in This Book

Aha Experience in Pittsburgh

This is akin to the feeling of an "Aha" epiphany. Once, I visited Pittsburgh. I drove through a tunnel from the far side of the mountain. Gradually, the tunnel entrance on the opposite side grew larger and larger. Upon emerging from the tunnel, the city of Pittsburgh unfolded before me. I vividly recall the panoramic view and the overwhelming sense of "Wow! Pittsburgh" that I experienced that day. I believe this sensation resembles the feeling of enlightenment and creativity that comes with an "Aha" moment.

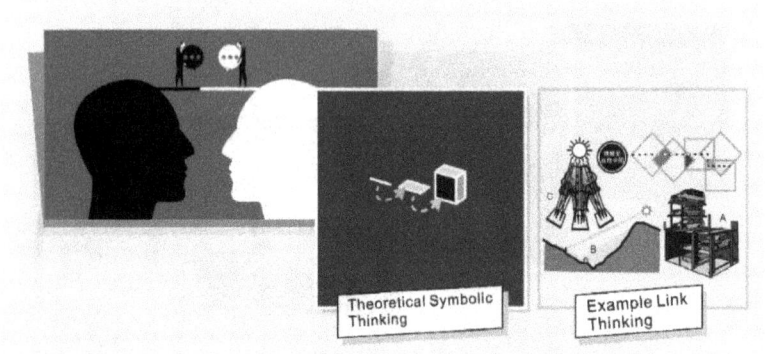

The Unique Design of This Book Alternates Between Black and Gray Backgrounds to Create Epiphanies

To foster an "Aha" effect in cross-border thinking, this book employs a unique design featuring alternating black and light gray backgrounds on its pages. The black background is dedicated to exploring abstract concepts such as theory, architecture, and operational methods. In contrast, the light gray background is used to provide real-world application examples, demonstrating how these principles are utilized across various fields. It is the seamless transition between abstract theory and concrete practice that is intended to evoke the "Aha" epiphany effect.

LEO YUAN, PH.D.

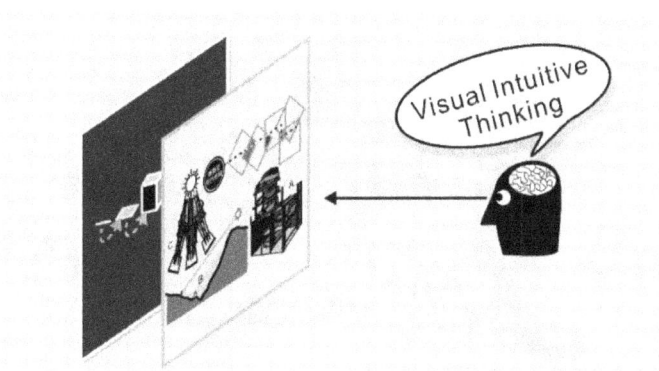

Visual Intuitive Thinking

This book primarily relies on visuals to facilitate visual thinking, enabling readers to swiftly grasp the approach to cross-border thinking. Visual thinking is emphasized for its three primary benefits:

Brain Activation: Viewing pictures engages over one-third of the brain, significantly enhancing cognitive efficiency during study and learning.

Clarity in Thinking: Visuals can clarify complex thinking frameworks that often confuse the mind, offering a clearer pathway to genuine understanding.

Enhanced Communication: Pictures are more accessible than text, aiding in effortless comprehension and fostering effective communication at a glance.

Read This Book at Any Time to Experience the "Aha" Epiphany Effect

The dissociation theory posits that the subconscious mind harbors vast amounts of unstructured information. When focused on a particular topic, thoughts circulate within the subconscious. Occasionally, two dissociated pieces of information collide, giving rise to what appears to be a plausible answer—this is termed inspiration.

This book offers numerous patterns and architectural symbols designed to foster serendipitous collisions. It's highly probable that, at some point, encountering a specific pattern, architectural symbol, or concise textual description could lead to an epiphany.

LEO YUAN, PH.D.

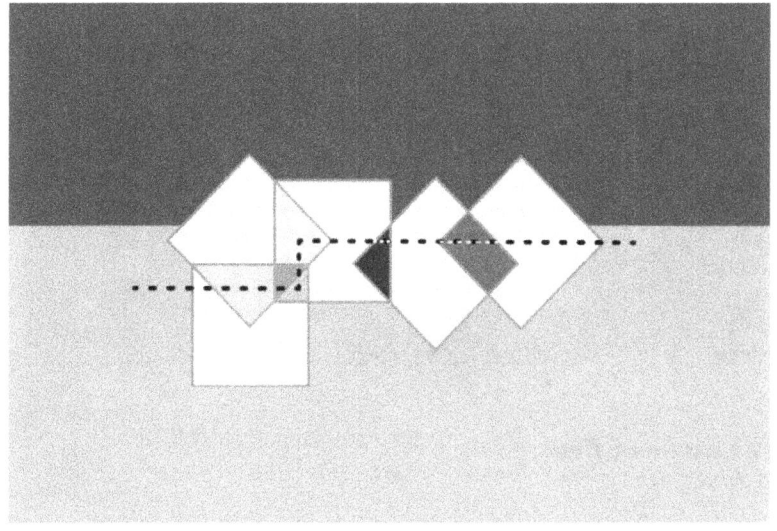

The Basic Principles of Cross-Border Thinking

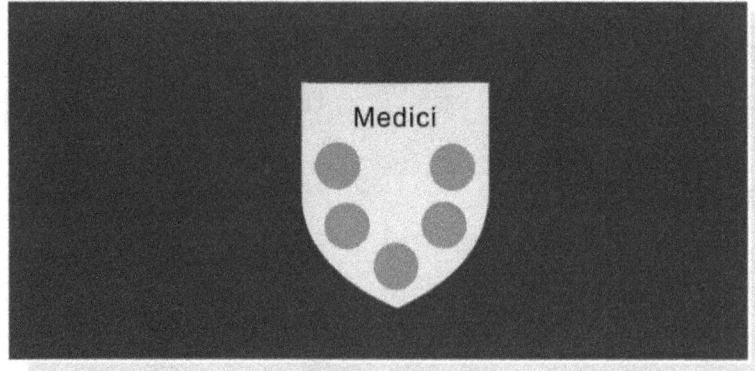

The Medici Effect

In the 15th century, in Italy, the Medici family, prominent in the banking industry in Florence, actively patronized culture and the arts. They created a platform that facilitated diverse activities and attracted elites from various backgrounds to gather and exchange ideas. This platform sparked a significant surge of creativity, ultimately establishing Florence as the epicenter of the Renaissance.

Frans Johansson authored the globally acclaimed book "The Medici Effect," which has inspired numerous entrepreneurs by illustrating how diverse fields and disciplines can intersect to generate innovative ideas and solutions.

LEO YUAN, PH.D.

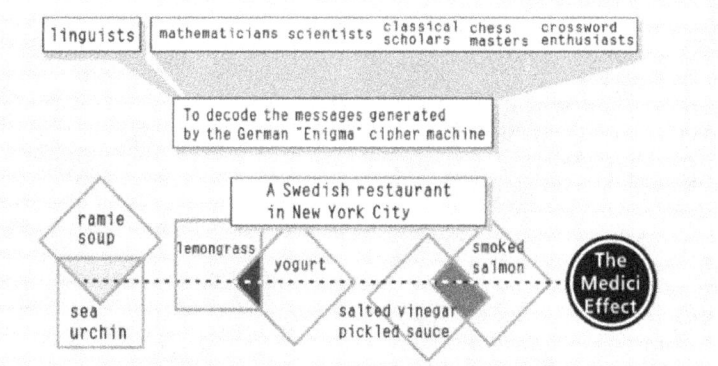

The Collision of Multiple Fields Often Sparks the Generation of New Ideas

In "The Medici Effect," it's mentioned that a Swedish restaurant in New York City hired Marcus Samuelsson as the chef. He innovatively combined Swedish cuisine with ingredients from various countries, resulting in creative dishes such as ramie soup with sea urchin, lemongrass yogurt, and salted vinegar pickled sauce with smoked salmon.

During World War II, to decode the messages generated by the German "Enigma" cipher machine, British intelligence assembled a highly sophisticated team. This team included linguists, mathematicians, scientists, classical scholars, chess masters, and crossword enthusiasts. Together, they successfully cracked the code, significantly influencing the outcome of naval battles during the war.

TRIZ, Theory of Inventive Problem Solving

Genrich Altshuller developed TRIZ, which stands for "Theory of Inventive Problem Solving" in English. Altshuller proposed that invention and creativity can be systematically learned and applied. He categorized the principles of invention into 39 engineering parameters and devised a matrix lookup table for easy reference.

TRIZ addresses technical contradictions where improving one aspect of a system may worsen another. In such scenarios, Altshuller identified and categorized common contradictions and provided solutions for each. These solutions typically fall into up to 4 main directions, utilizing a total of 40 invention principles.

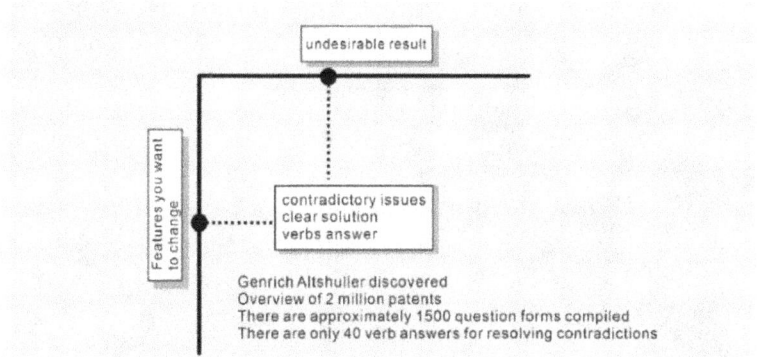

40 Invention Principles to Solve Most Problems

Genrich Altshuller examined approximately 2 million patents and identified around 1,500 common problem patterns. From this vast dataset, he distilled these patterns into just 40 invention principles within his Theory of Inventive Problem Solving (TRIZ). These principles address technical conflicts where improving one aspect of a system may worsen another.

TRIZ provides a systematic approach to solving invention problems, drawing from extensive patent data to offer effective solutions. Mastery of TRIZ enables individuals to accelerate the invention process and achieve high-quality innovative products efficiently. This methodology highlights the importance of structured thinking and systematic analysis in overcoming complex challenges across various industries.

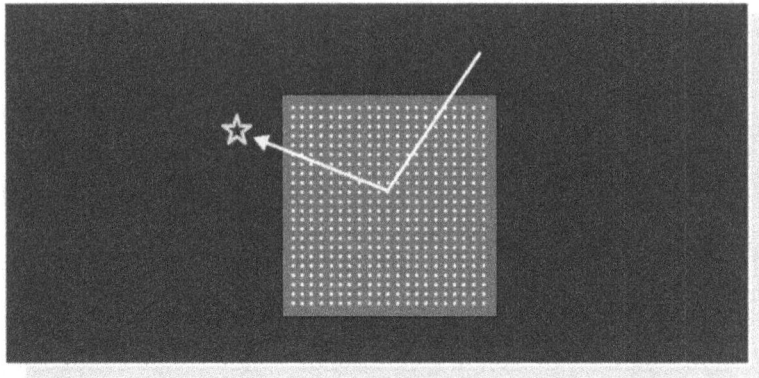

Trigger Concepts Can Ignite Creativity

Roger von Oech introduced Trigger Concepts as a creative development method involving the random selection of words. This approach encourages individuals to associate various questions and answers with the chosen word, often leading to unexpected connections and ideas that wouldn't typically arise. When encountering a trigger word, it acts like pulling a trigger in your mind, disrupting habitual thinking patterns and prompting you to explore new associations and possibilities. This method aims to stimulate creativity and generate innovative ideas or directions for development.

LEO YUAN, PH.D.

God	safety	liquid	skeleton	nose	fence	flag
trap	key	shadow	valley	hoe	lawyer	temple
compass	moon	liver	maze	stamp	bed board	cave
foam	sand	ocean	tunnel	radar	Rubbish	television
game	stairs	**bread**	algebra	skin	gender	web page
look	satellite		rainbow	food	map	flying birds
table	disc	sketch	ice cubes	coat	passport	heart
target	bread	Soap	meteor	**wine**	house	eye
oval	croissant	pen	perfume		piano	sharp sword
port	bagel	call	Pope	family	penguin	money
garden	powder	the way	insect	magnet	wine	memory
hammer	project	camera	nail	vegetable	desert	molecular
Body	treasure	Big drum	vase	burnt	cell	computer
flame	hair	frog	machine	roots	engine	thigh

Selecting a Word at Random Can Spark a Cascade of Extended Ideas

When you close your eyes and point to "bread" with your finger, consider the problem you are currently thinking about, brainstorm something related to the concept of 'bread,' and explore it. For instance: What types of bread exist? Besides water, what other liquids can bread absorb? "Good land is the cultivator's bread." "Beer is the bread of drunkards." "Countries with low taxes are bread for new businesses."

Use the "Trigger Concepts" method to select "bread" and make broader associations to uncover new concepts or areas that you haven't explored before. This approach may aid in developing ideas or solving problems.

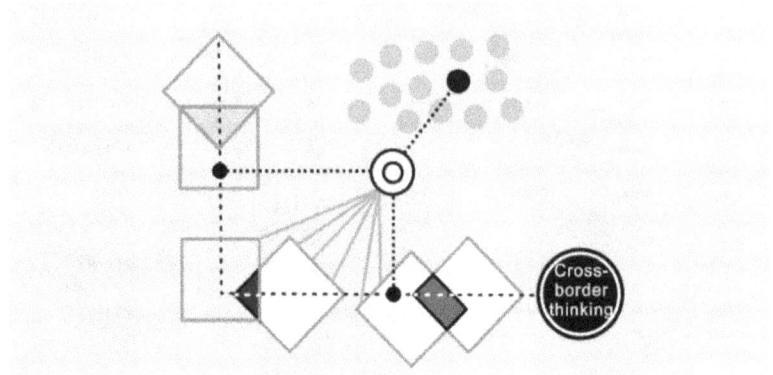

Three Creative Theories Illustrate Cross-Border Thinking

The architecture diagram for cross-border thinking can become quite complex when illustrated, given the numerous ways to engage in cross-border activities. For instance, the combination method of the Medici approach, TRIZ's conflict resolution, and Trigger Concepts' random word selection illustrate the integration of three distinct creative methodologies, creating a complex structure.

However, cross-border thinking can be simplified to a single operational principle that is applicable across various fields. By reading the graphical explanations provided in this book, cross-border thinking can naturally develop.

LEO YUAN, PH.D.

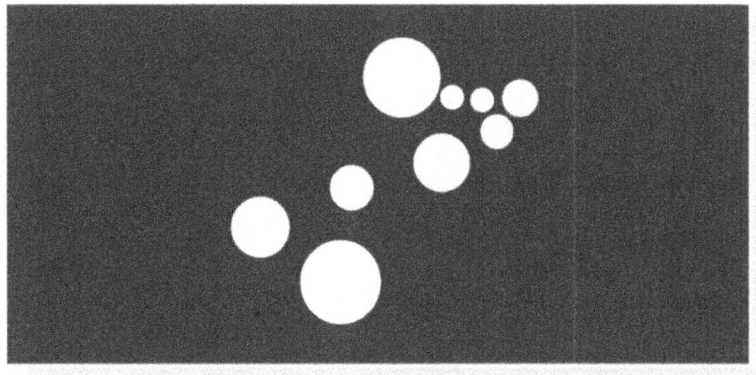

Seems Unrelated, But Actually, They Are Related

What do these dots mean? Observing their arrangement, it appears that there are one or two underlying principles at play. It seems as though there is a force pulling them, causing them to align along an invisible "curve".

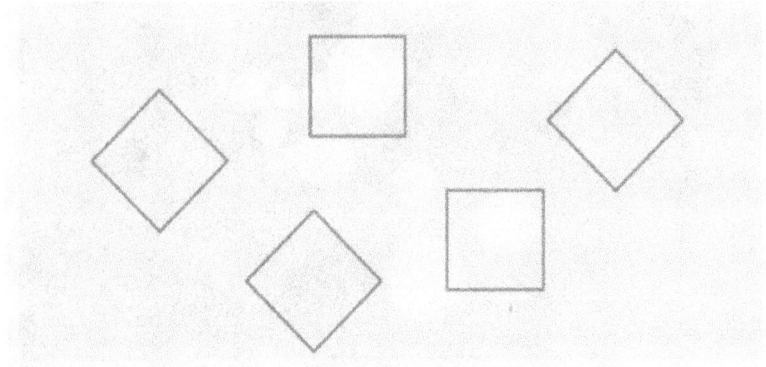

There is a Connection Between Things

At first glance, everything we see may appear unrelated to each other, but each thing operates according to certain principles that are often similar or consistent with one another. Despite their independent appearances, there is underlying unity in their operation.

LEO YUAN, PH.D.

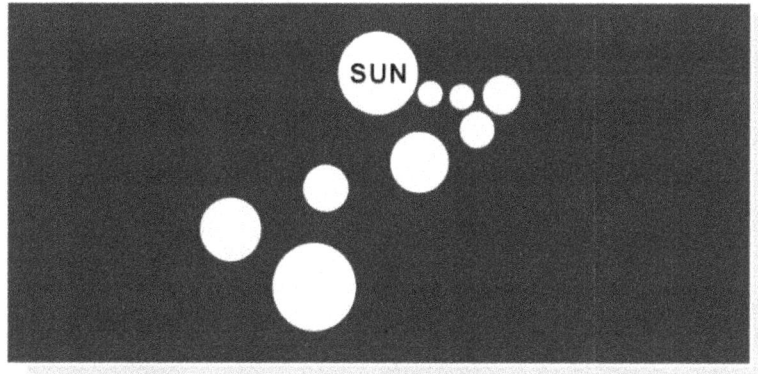

Just One Symbol Can Reveal a Truth

If "SUN" is marked at the top, then these objects share a collective association. They might represent planets, and their arrangement likely mirrors the orbits within the solar system.

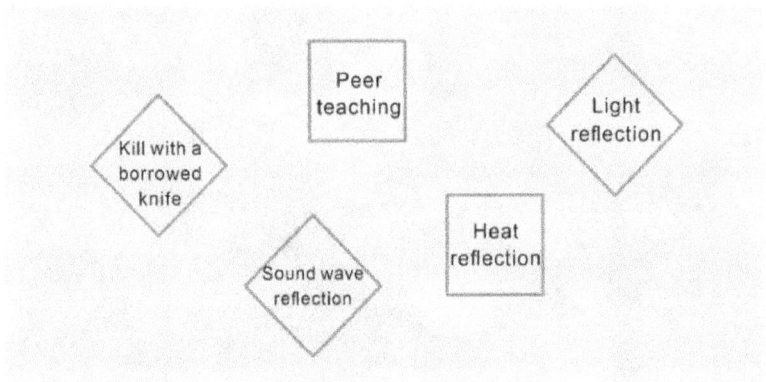

Different Types of Representation, But They Imply the Same Principle

Although "Kill with a borrowed knife" and "Peer teaching" are two different concepts, they operate on the same principle, similar to sound waves, light, and heat reflection. Upon careful consideration, do both "Kill with a borrowed knife" and "Peer teaching" operate based on the principle of 'reflection'?

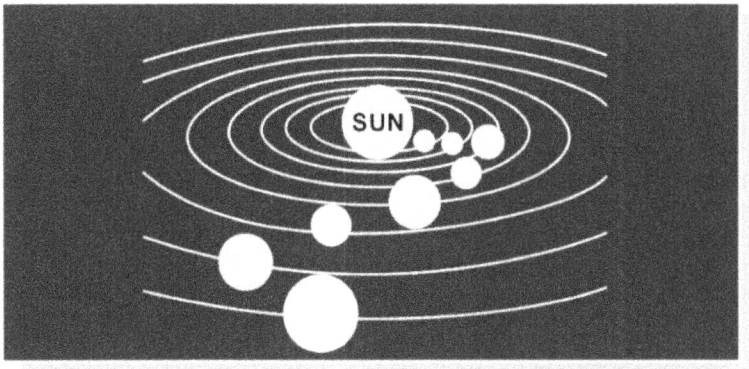

The Gravity of the Solar System Determines the Orbits of the Planets

When the lines of planetary orbits are drawn, the dots have a reason to be related to each other. Therefore, everything should share similarities. This could include appearance, operational modes, material characteristics, conveying equipment, and more. By closely observing the details and structures of each item, you will discover their similarities and commonalities with other things.

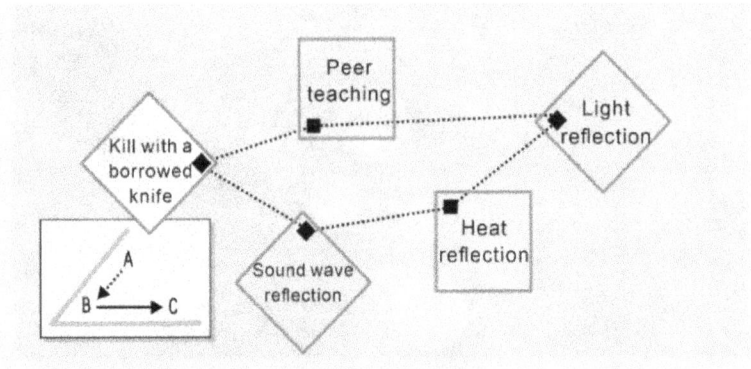

Reflective Operation is Present in Everything

If A wants to kill C, he does so through the hands of B. The operating principle of "Kill with a borrowed knife" is similar to that of "Peer teaching". A teacher aims to impart knowledge to students and achieve optimal results. Good students become "pupil teachers" who assist in teaching. Thus, both methods operate on the same principle.

When observing light reflection frequently, attempt to apply this "reflection" to various situations and gradually develop this foundational skill of cross-border thinking.

LEO YUAN, PH.D.

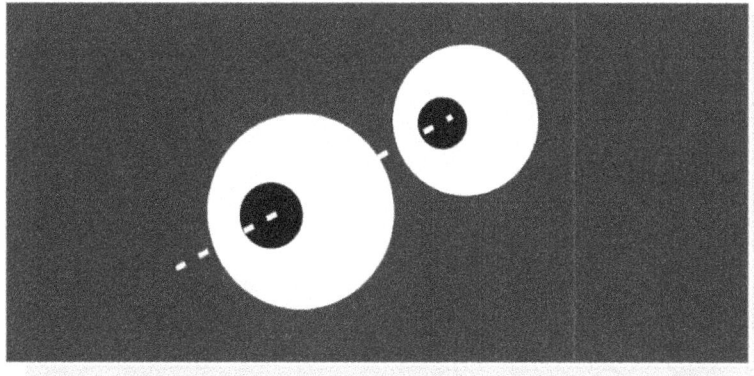

Every Object Implies a Pathway Through Which They Can Communicate with Each Other

Imagine two spheres with a hole passing through each of them. At a specific angle, this hole can connect to the next sphere.

This concept is called interoperability. The structure of each sphere is diverse and complex, yet there should be a common element shared with other spheres, allowing them to connect and communicate with each other.

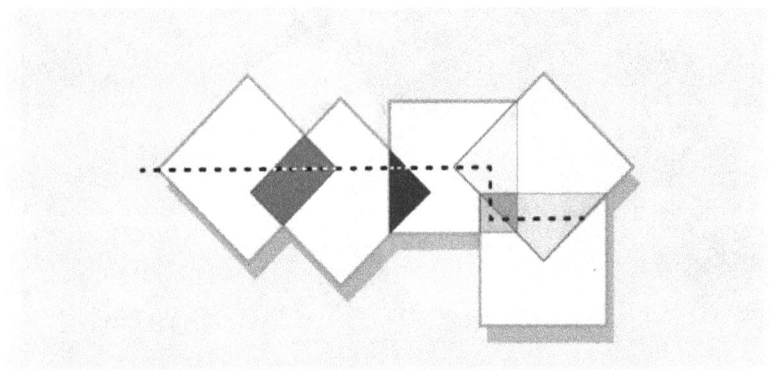

The Intersection is What Two Shapes Have in Common

If two things share the same operating principle, then there is overlap. Sometimes multiple things operate according to the same principle or have multiple principles simultaneously. Everything is interconnected.
Once you understand how this correlation functions, you can transition from one thing to the next.

LEO YUAN, PH.D.

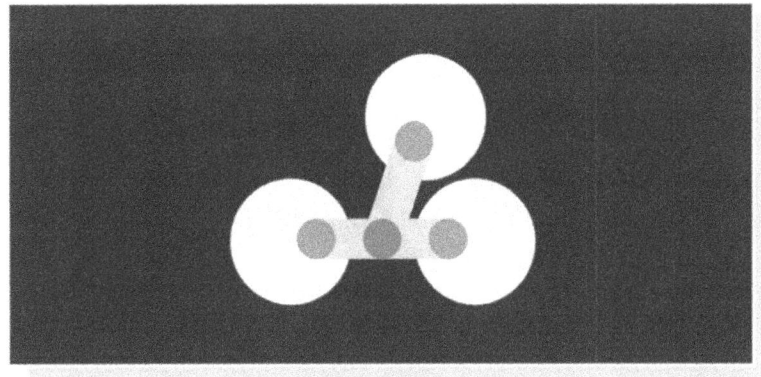

If You Encounter Three Random Objects, You Should Be Able to Identify Their Intersection

The three spheres all operate on the same principle, so there is an intersection. It's akin to tying three spheres together with a rope. Conversely, if you establish an operating principle and apply it to other things, or use this principle to analyze other objects, you will often discover items that share this operating principle.

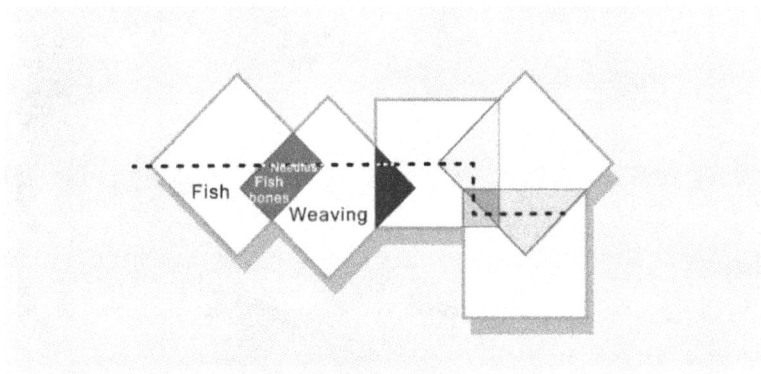

Are Fish and Weaving Related?

The common operating principle between fish and weaving is spikes. The spikes of fish refer to fish bones, which form the skeleton that supports the fish's body; in weaving, needles are essential tools. When ancient people ate fish and observed the sharp fish bones, they might have been inspired to use sharp stones for hunting or to sharpen needles for sewing clothes. Cross-border thinking can enhance life in similar ways. It serves as a fundamental cornerstone for the advancement of human civilization.

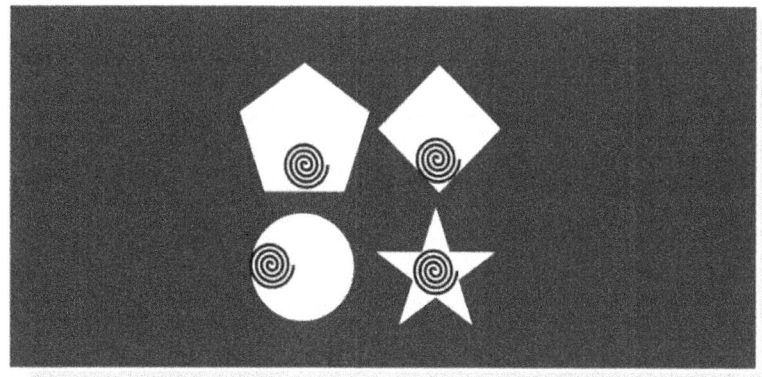

One Truth Connects Many Things: The Benefits of Cross-Border Thinking

Different things often share the same operating principle. When intelligent people discover this principle, they can associate and apply it. When faced with a problem, a potential solution may lie in an unexpected place, utilizing its operating principle.

Archimedes was troubled by the problem of verifying whether a crown made of pure gold had been adulterated with silver. Unexpectedly, while taking a bath at home and observing the water overflowing, he suddenly conceived a solution. This demonstrates that two seemingly unrelated things may share the same operating principle.

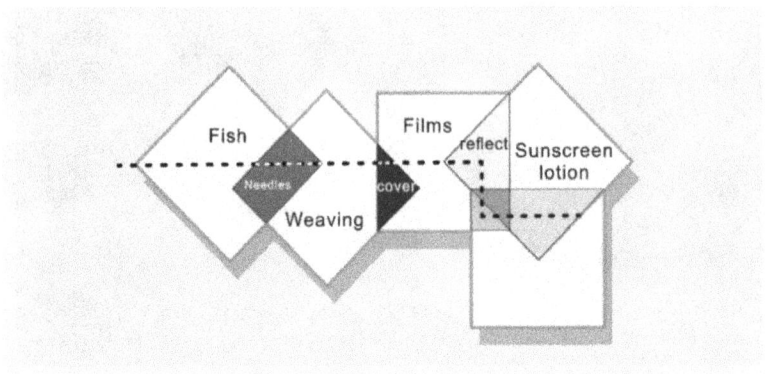

Cross-Border Thinking Can Also Be Applied to Solitaire

The common feature between fish and weaving is needles. Needle-like fish bones form the skeleton of a fish's body, while needles are essential tools in weaving. When fabric covers the body, one might think of using a film to cover objects. Films serve various purposes such as waterproof breathable films, UV-reflective films, and more. If a film can reflect UV rays, one might consider it akin to sunscreen lotion when applied to the skin.

By harnessing this associative power, you can observe the objects around you and embark on an associative journey while waiting for the bus, soaking in a hot spring, or sitting in a cafe waiting for someone.

LEO YUAN, PH.D.

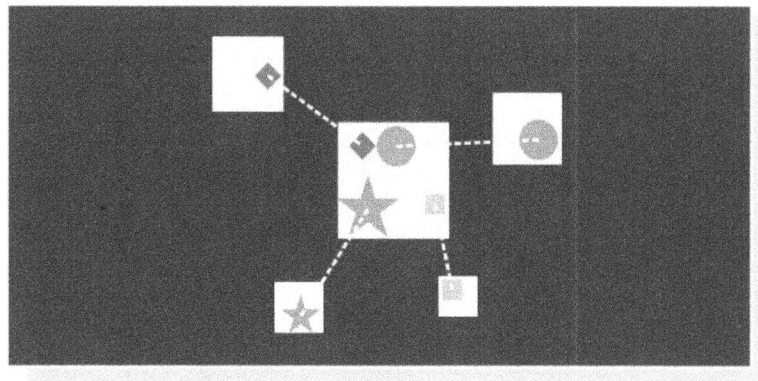

Every Object Contains Many Elements

The connection between each thing and other things does not rely solely on one operating principle. Each object is a complex amalgamation of organic and inorganic physical interactions and chemical reactions, with multiple operations at play. Through human association, exploration, analysis, and other forms of thinking, one can discover numerous similar operating principles.

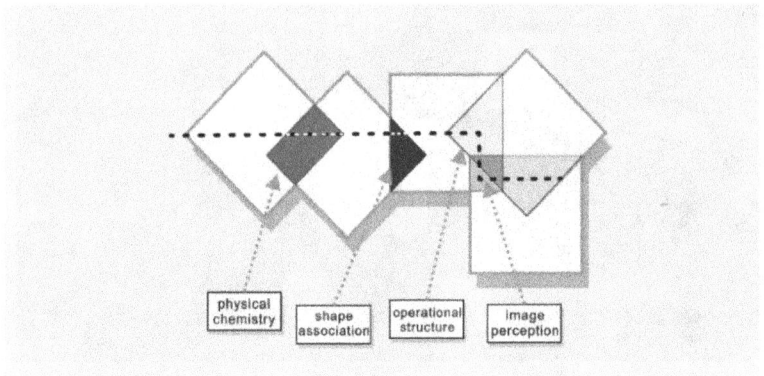

From Your Professional Perspective, You Can Also Engage in Cross-Border Thinking

Rational individuals will focus on the operating principles of physical effects or chemical reactions in each object. Those interested in art and design often associate with appearance and shape, and their knowledge of animals and plants enhances these associations. Engineers in mechanical or civil fields possess deep insights into operational structures.

Anyone with the desire and motivation to engage in cross-border thinking can become adept at identifying interoperable operating principles through regular practice. By using the aforementioned four approaches—physical chemistry, shape association, operational structure, and image perception—one can uncover numerous operating principles.

LEO YUAN, PH.D.

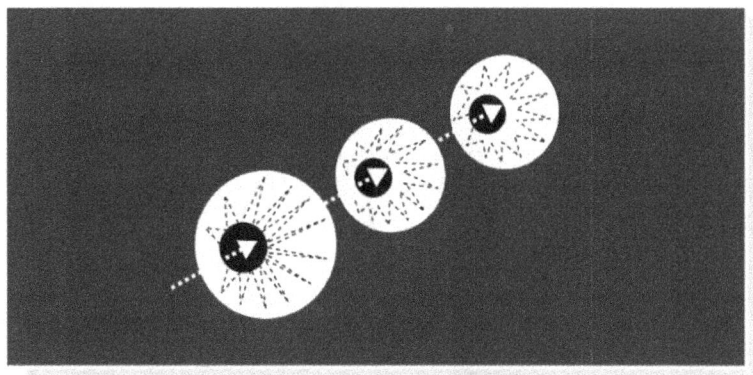

Even Without a Common Principle, It Can Still Be Applied

Imagine a force striking a sphere, causing an explosion inside or initiating internal flow. Each time it encounters a sphere, it continues to proliferate inside and merges with it to generate a new idea.

If your thinking can be like this, you can establish a theme or an operating principle and directly apply it to any object. If the object does not align with your established theme, it's best to simply apply the theme directly. Combine it with the object and see if you can create something new.

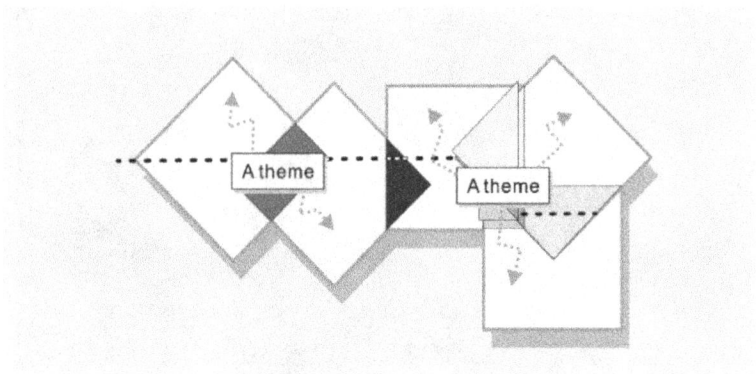

Trigger Concepts Can Truly Serve as Bullets for Fostering Connections

Utilize Trigger Concepts to discover a word, establish a theme yourself, or identify an operating principle. Apply it directly to one thing and commence the process of combining it to generate new concepts.

Innovation, by definition, involves something unexpected. How does it achieve this?

The word uncovered using Trigger Concepts may not initially come to mind, hence it starts off as unexpected. There's a high probability that this word can be applied to anything. By combining these elements, you can create new products that surprise everyone.

LEO YUAN, PH.D.

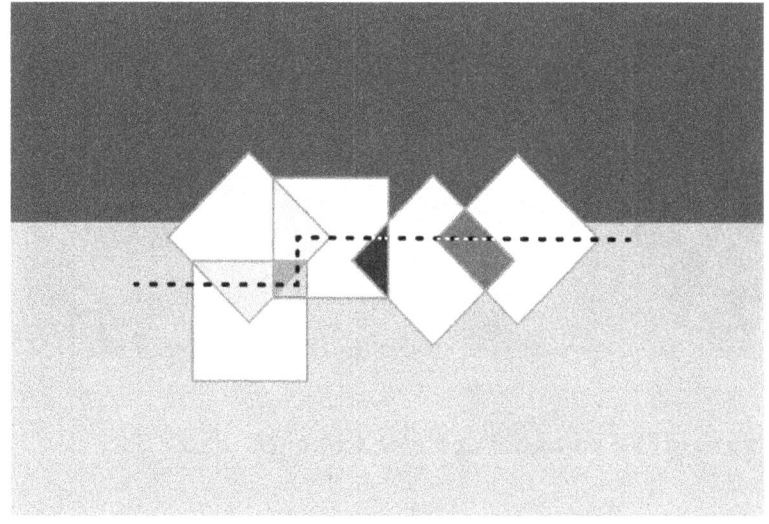

Invention Principles Topic

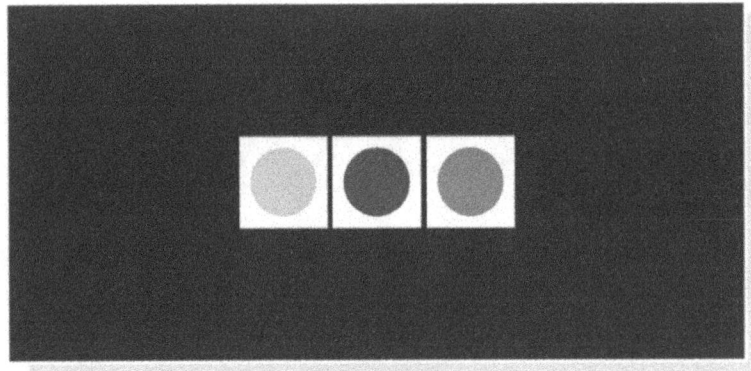

Explore The Potential of Color Changes

Color Changes: Altering the color of an object or system to enhance its value or detect issues.
Specific operations:
1. Change the color of an object or its surroundings.
2. Adjust the transparency of an object or its surroundings.
3. Use color additives to observe objects or processes that are difficult to perceive.
4. Reapply luminescent tracking elements if these additives are already in use.
This is the 32nd invention principle proposed by TRIZ for problem-solving.

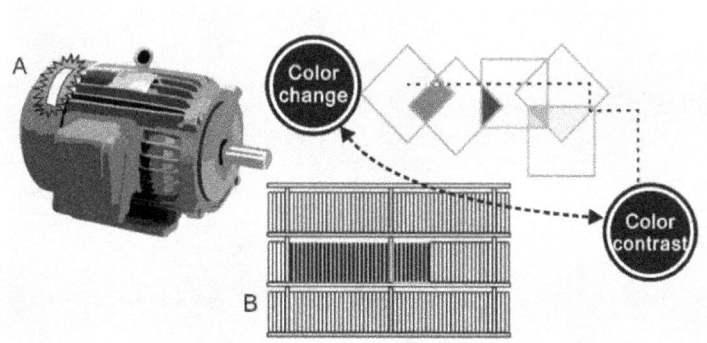

Colors That Can Solve Problems or Create Business Opportunities

A: Place a sticker on the motor that changes color when exposed to heat. When the motor overheats and the sticker changes color, the manager will know there is a problem with the motor.

B: Color change can also be utilized for contrast. In a bookstore filled with books, if there is a series with black covers, placing 20 or 30 of these books together will create a large black area visible from a distance. This catches the eye of readers, piquing their curiosity enough to browse through them.

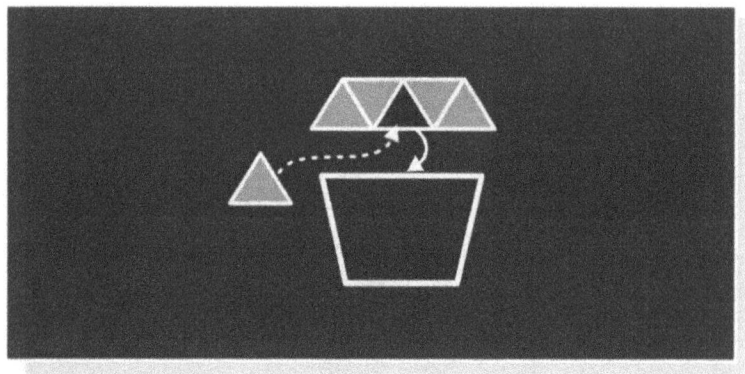

Discarding and Recovering: Giving Products New Life

Discarding and Recovering combines two principles—discarding and regeneration—into one. The discarding principle involves removing something from the system, while the regeneration principle focuses on restoring and reusing something within the system.

Specific operations:

1. When the object has completed its function or is no longer useful, discard, modify, decompose, or dissipate it.
2. Directly restore exhausted parts or objects.

This is the 34th invention principle proposed by TRIZ for problem-solving.

LEO YUAN, PH.D.

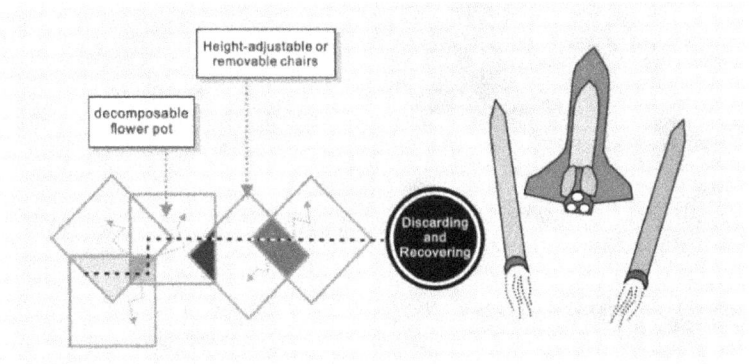

Decompose, Dismantle, Disappear, And Then Be Reborn

1. After the rocket thruster successfully completes its voyage phase and exhausts its fuel, it is jettisoned to allow the spacecraft or satellite to enter space.

2. Use flowerpots made of materials that can decompose through microorganisms and place them in the soil for planting flowers and plants. Over time, the flowerpots will naturally decompose and integrate with the soil. There is no need to dig them out or remove them.

3. Design the four legs of children's chairs to be segmented. Regardless of their height, children can sit on them. The legs can be disassembled or added to as needed.

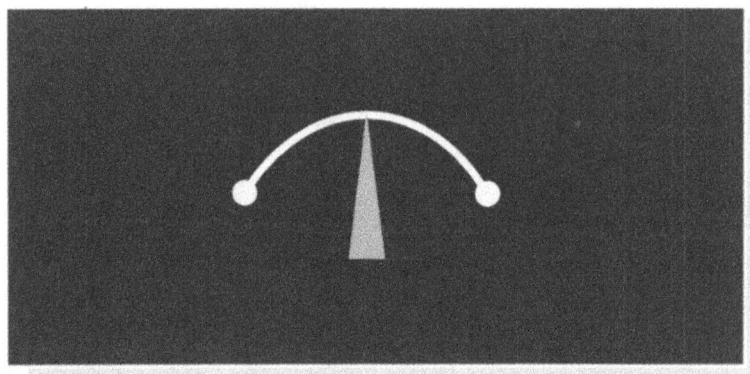

Another Force, Counterweight

Counterweight: Balance and compensate in equal amounts to achieve even distribution. If there is an issue with the weight of an object or system, something that provides lift can be combined to solve the problem of gravitational balance; alternatively, other energy resources can be utilized.
Specific operations:
1. Connect another object with lifting force to compensate for the weight of the object.
2. Utilize aerodynamic or hydraulic power from the environment to compensate for the weight of the object.
This is the eighth invention principle proposed by TRIZ for problem-solving.

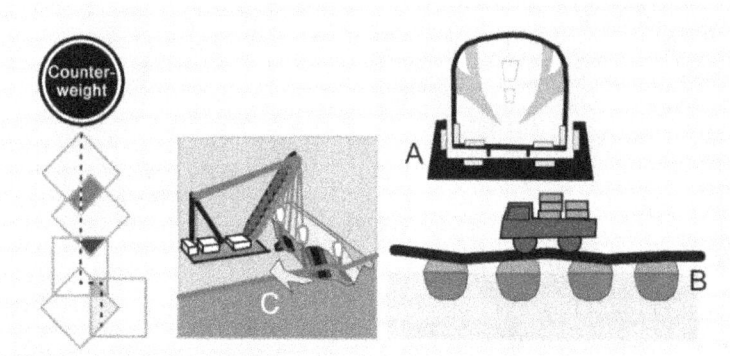

Using Counterweight to Solve Problems with Large Objects

A: In a maglev train, the electromagnet under the vehicle and the electromagnet in the track generate identical magnetic fields. This causes the vehicle to levitate due to repulsive magnetic forces, with its only resistance being air resistance.

B: Floating bridge: Pontoons support a continuous bridge deck for temporary passage of pedestrians and vehicles.

C: Salvaging a sunken ship involves using a large crane on a tugboat to lift the ship, while air bags are installed to utilize buoyancy for additional upward force to help bring the ship back to a normal upright position.

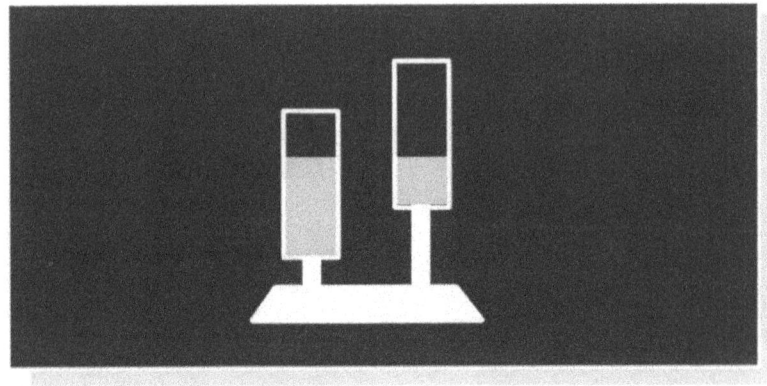

When The Force and Target Are at Different Heights, Equipotentiality is Required

Equipotentiality: Establishing continuous and fully connected unions and relationships.
Specific operation: Modify the working conditions so that the object does not need to be lifted or lowered.
This is the 12th invention principle proposed by TRIZ for solving problems.

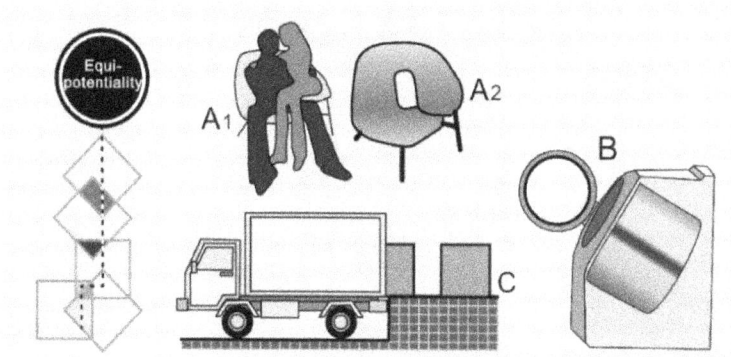

Your Working Height Equals the Target Object

A: When a couple of different heights embrace each other, specially designed seats of varying heights make it easier for them to converse.

B: The opening of the drum-type washing machine is slanted and positioned at waist height, making it easier to load and unload clothes.

C: Truck unloading platform: The working areas for unloading trucks and replenishing the warehouse are at the same height. This allows goods to be moved horizontally without the need for vertical lifting.

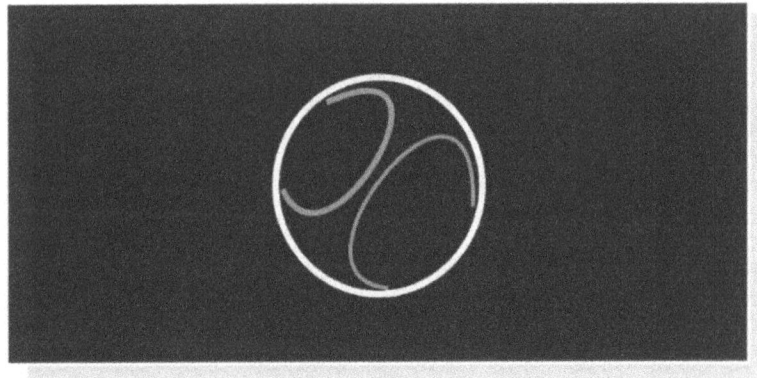

Use Spheres Instead of Planes and Curves Instead of Straight Lines

Spheroidality: Utilizing the characteristics of curves or spherical surfaces to replace straight-line properties; employing curved surfaces such as rotating rollers, cams, balls, etc., instead of linear motion.

Specific operations:

1. Substitute linear components or planes with curves, and replace cubes with spheres.
2. Employ rollers, balls, and spirals.
3. Replace linear motion with rotational motion or utilize centrifugal force.

This is the 14th invention principle proposed by TRIZ for problem-solving.

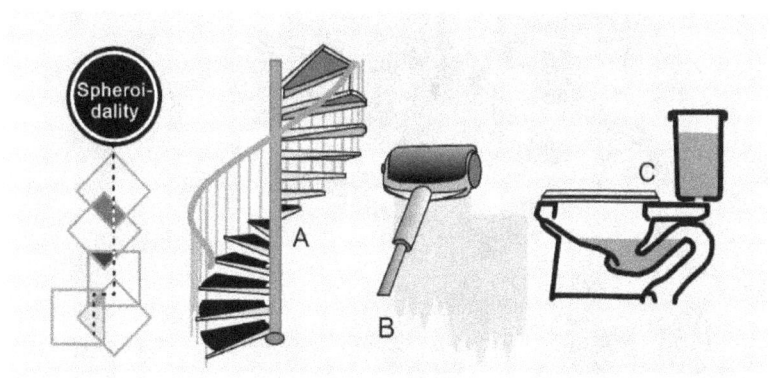

Curved Surfaces and Circular Designs Are Sometimes Preferable to Use

A: Spiral staircase.
B: Roller paintbrush.
C: The clever design of the toilet flush utilizes curved contours to retain a small section of water, preventing cockroaches from entering the house through the bottom water pipe.

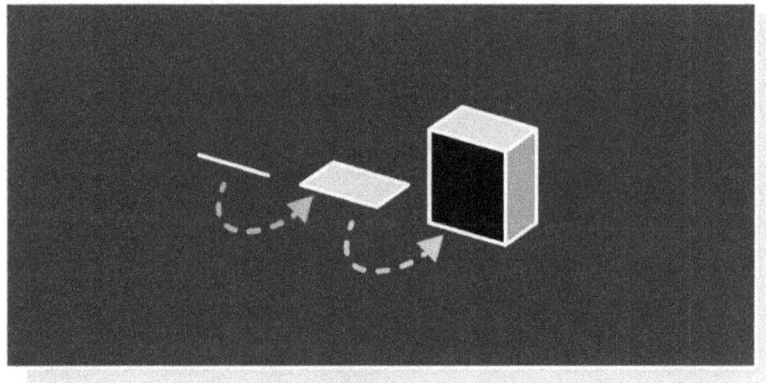

Exploring The Possibilities of Another Dimension

Another Dimension: Altering the orientation of a linear system from vertical to horizontal, horizontal to diagonal, or horizontal to vertical. Transforming a one-dimensional motion or object into a two-dimensional motion or object, or evolving a two-dimensional motion or object into a three-dimensional one.

Specific operations:
1. Utilize multi-layer combinations instead of single layers.
2. Tilt the object.
3. Project an image onto adjacent areas or onto the opposite side of the object.

This is the 17th invention principle proposed by TRIZ for problem-solving.

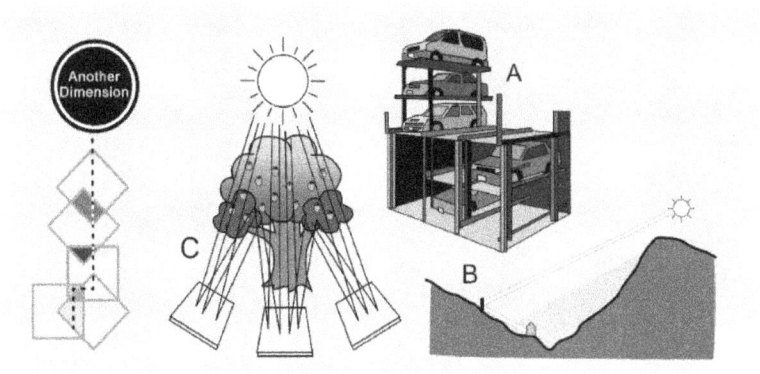

Utilize Various Physical Laws to Guide You to Another Space

A: Advance to a higher level and design mechanical parking spaces two floors above or below ground level.

B: To resolve the issue of the back of the house not receiving sunlight, strategically reflect sunlight from an appropriate location.

C: If apple trees become overly dense and block sunlight, install reflective panels on the ground to ensure apples beneath the dense foliage receive adequate sunlight.

Speed is Also a Key Element in Problem Solving

Skipping: When something malfunctions at a specific speed, acceleration is necessary; meaning, analyze the causes of detrimental functions, events, and conditions to discover ways to modify speed. Sometimes, employing high speed to execute an action can eliminate harmful side effects.
Specific operations: Execute harmful or risky operations at high speeds. This is the 21st invention principle proposed by TRIZ that can solve problems.

LEO YUAN, PH.D.

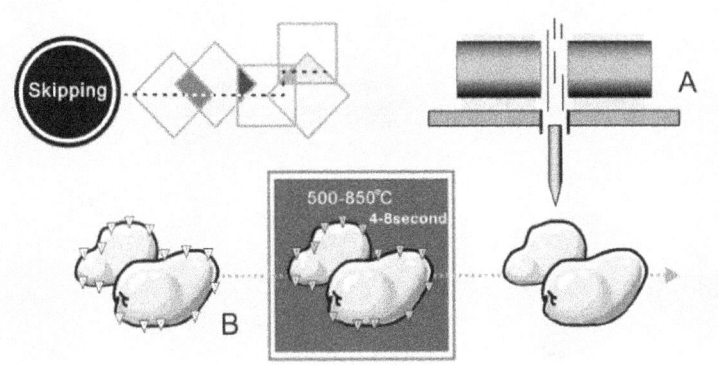

Quick Movements Can Prevent the Target from Reacting in Time

A: In a thin-walled, large-diameter plastic pipe, cutting swiftly with a slicing knife prevents the pipe from deforming.

B: Potatoes are prone to rot if bacteria adhere to them. While heating can remove bacteria, overheating will cook the potatoes. Rapid action can solve this problem effectively. The furnace is set to a high temperature of 500-850 degrees Celsius, and the potatoes are quickly inserted and removed within 4 to 8 seconds. This process eliminates all bacteria on the potato surface without affecting the interior.

The Functions You Generate Can Also Solve Your Own Problems

Self-Service: Utilize the primary functions or operations of the system to autonomously perform related functions or operations. Self-service assumes an automatic feedback mechanism instead of requiring a separate setup for feedback.
Specific Operations:
1. Enable the object to conduct self-replenishment and repair operations.
2. Minimize material and energy waste.
This is the 25th invention principle proposed by TRIZ that addresses problem-solving.

LEO YUAN, PH.D.

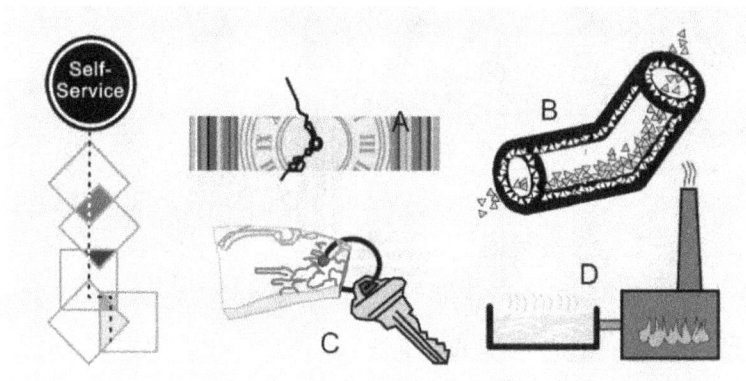

The Advantages of Objects Can Still Be Utilized Until the Last Moment

A: Ancient clock gears or certain metal components can be repurposed as decorative elements in modern clocks.

B: To prevent hard substances from causing abrasion on the inner surface of a pipe, grind these substances and apply them evenly to the pipe's interior. This method ensures uniform hardness and significantly reduces wear.

C: Broken pieces of ancient porcelain can be fashioned into decorative keychains.

D: A steel plant or incinerator equipped with thermal heating can transfer excess heat energy to a nearby swimming pool, turning it into a heated pool.

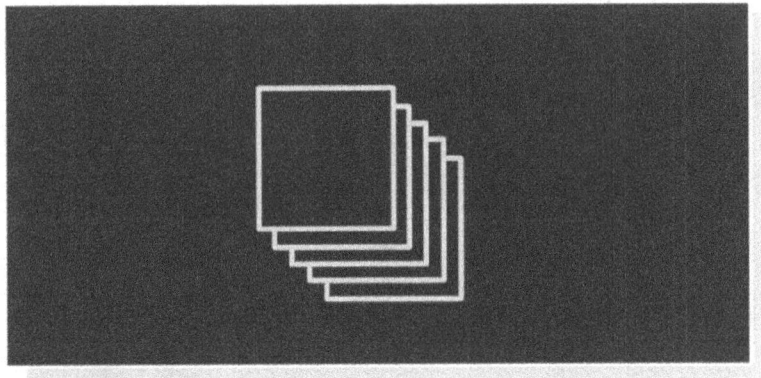

Copying to Obtain Larger Amounts of Resources

Copying: Substituting something valuable with a replica or model; that is, finding and utilizing easy-to-obtain, low-cost, and durable replicas.

Specific operations:

1. Use simple, inexpensive replicas to replace complex, expensive, fragile, or inconvenient objects for operation.
2. Replace an object or system with an optical replica, optical image, or scale that can be used to reduce or enlarge the image.
3. Replace visible light copying with infrared or ultraviolet copying.

This is the 26th invention principle proposed by TRIZ for solving problems.

LEO YUAN, PH.D.

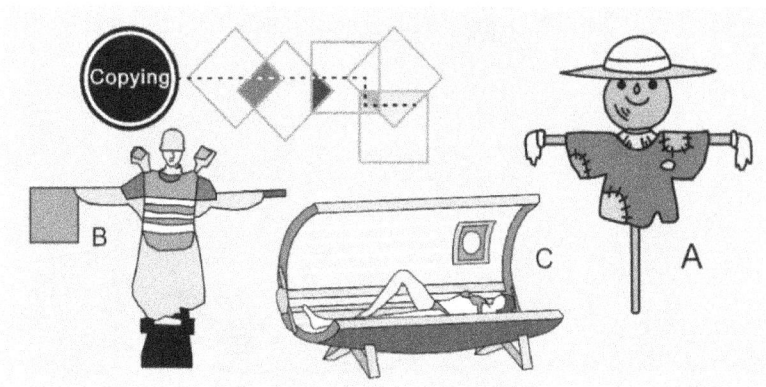

Imitating and Copying Natural Phenomena or Human Events to Save Effort

A: The scarecrow replaces the farmer to protect the rice in the field.

B: The traffic conductor doll resembles a staff member from a distance.

C: An indoor tanning machine that mimics the sun's ultraviolet rays and directly irradiates the whole body.

Advancing the Medici Fusion

Pneumatics and Hydraulics: Using Pressure to Design Operational Systems

Pneumatics and hydraulics involve the use of gases or liquids to replace components or functions within a system.
Specific Operations:
1. Replace solid parts of an object with gas or liquid.
2. Use air or fluid to expand, compress, or cushion parts.
This is the 29th invention principle proposed by TRIZ to solve problems.

LEO YUAN, PH.D.

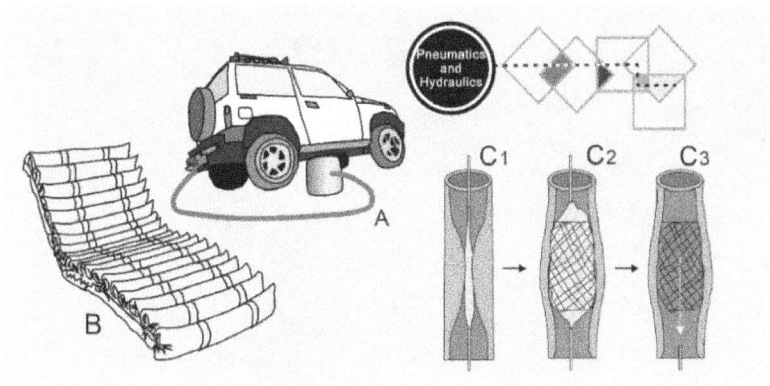

Increased Pressure Can Save Effort, Support The Body, or Save Lives

A: An inflatable jack uses exhaust gas from the exhaust pipe for inflation.
B: An air mattress can be easily carried and inflated when needed.
C: For a blocked heart blood vessel, a stent is installed: C1: The stent is first introduced into the blocked blood vessel. C2: It is expanded using a balloon. C3: The catheter is then withdrawn.

Homogeneity: Objects or Substances Made from The Same Materials Are Most Harmonious with Each Other

Homogeneity: Objects or substances that interact with each other should ideally be composed of the same materials, raw materials, or information. This principle suggests seeking homogeneous compositions within a system or applying it across various levels of materials, energy, information, and interactions.

Specific operation: Ensure that objects interact with materials that are of the same composition or exhibit similar behavior.

This is the 33rd invention principle proposed by TRIZ for solving problems.

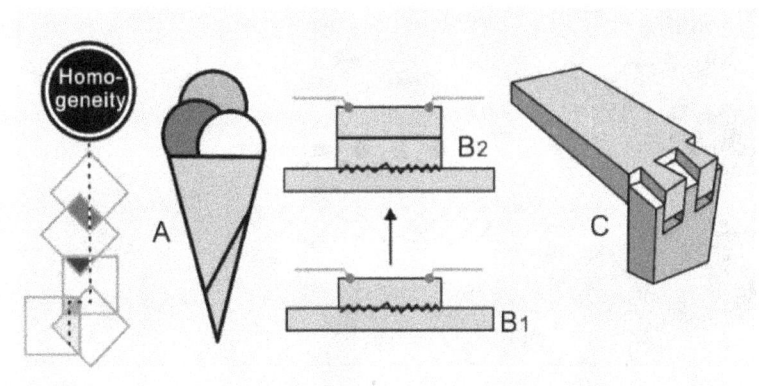

All Are Made from The Same Substance, And Sometimes They Can All Be Eaten

A: Edible cone cups use edible materials such as cups or cookies.

B: B1: The operation of the upper chip generates heat. The thermal expansion coefficient of the lower lead frame and the chip is different, which causes thermal strain on the chip; B2: Adding another chip in the middle reduces the thermal strain on the top chip.

C: Assembled using tenon joints, wooden furniture does not require a single iron nail.

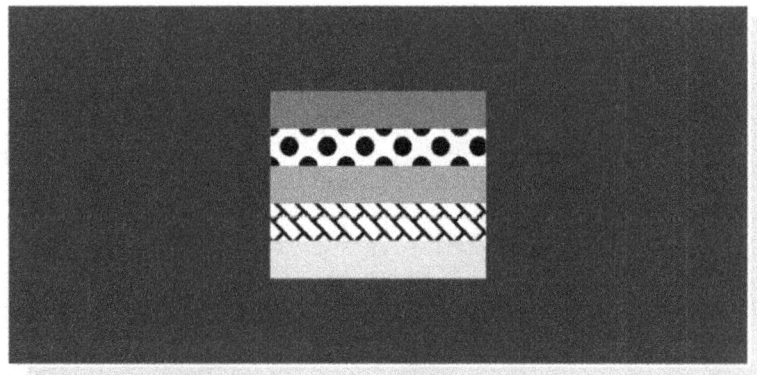

Composite Materials: Composite Structures and Innovative Uses

Composite Materials: Transforming uniform material structures into composite structures implies imbuing them with new material properties. This concept generally involves creating novel material conditions by replacing homogeneous materials with synthetic alternatives.

This principle represents the 40th invention principle proposed by TRIZ, aimed at solving various problems.

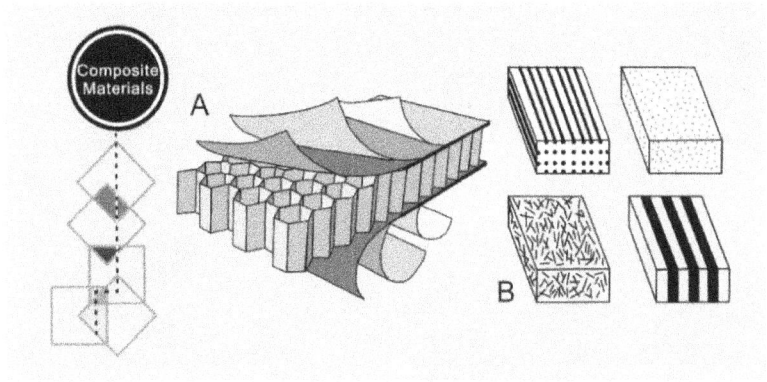

The Performance of Composite Materials is Beyond Imagination

A: The honeycomb structure of sandwich plywood can also be utilized for aircraft wings.

B: Wooden boards made from composite wood, handmade soaps crafted from various raw materials, gummy candies prepared from a mix of ingredients, etc. The composite approach can diversify products and, at times, enhance their characteristics or functions.

Intermediary, Providing Relief or Strengthening Connections

Intermediary: Utilizing easily removable intermediaries or protocols to temporarily link incompatible groups, events, or conditions.

Specific operations: Use an intermediate object to convert or complete an action. Temporarily attach one object to another to facilitate its removal.

This is the 24th invention principle proposed by TRIZ that can solve problems.

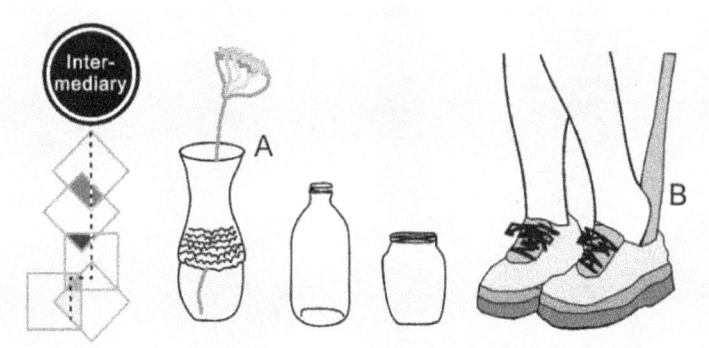

It Can Be Used as a Decorative or Buffering Intermediary

A: Arranging flowers in ordinary glass vases isn't very attractive, so we designed an intermediary—a rubber cover with patterns for the vase—to enhance its appearance.

B: A shoehorn. Are there other common daily necessities similar to shoehorns that also serve as intermediaries?

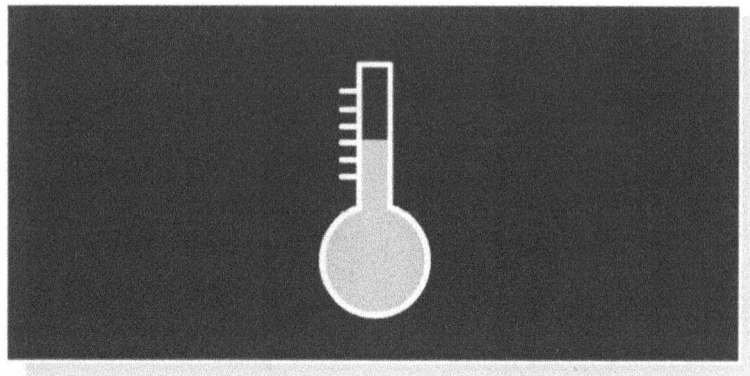

Thermal Expansion: Generates Outward Pressure

Thermal Expansion: Convert thermal energy into mechanical action; in other words, use the changes produced after heating to achieve the desired function. Specific operations:
1. Use heat to expand or contract materials.
2. Utilize materials with different thermal expansion coefficients.

This is the 37th invention principle proposed by TRIZ that can solve problems.

LEO YUAN, PH.D.

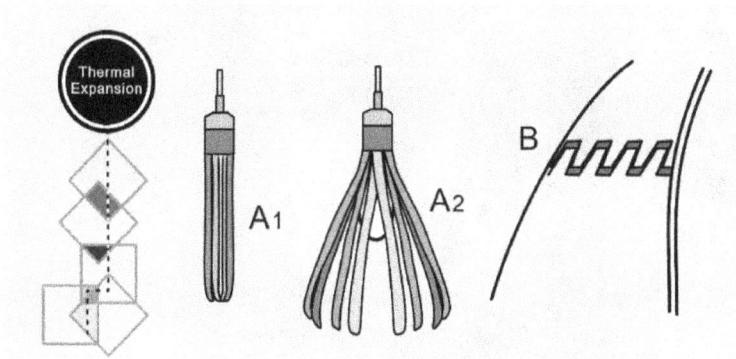

With Thermal Expansion, Life Becomes More Enjoyable and Smoother

A: A1: Use many thin aluminum sheets to make a lamp. After turning on the light (A2), the heat from the bulb causes the aluminum sheets to expand.
B: In winter, when temperatures are low, the bridge contracts and shortens, enlarging the gaps in the expansion joints. Conversely, thermal expansion in summer makes the expansion joints smaller.

Phase Transitions Alter States, Transforming Functionality

Phase Transition: Utilize material or environmental phase changes to effect or alter systems; in essence, apply phase transition to generate useful forces like gas, endothermic, exothermic reactions, and volume changes. Typical phase transitions include gas to liquid, liquid to solid, and gas to solid.
Specific operations:
1. Achieve specific effects during material state changes.
2. Achieve effective growth during the phase transformation process of matter; for example, heat release or absorption during volume change processes.
This is the 36th invention principle proposed by TRIZ for problem-solving.

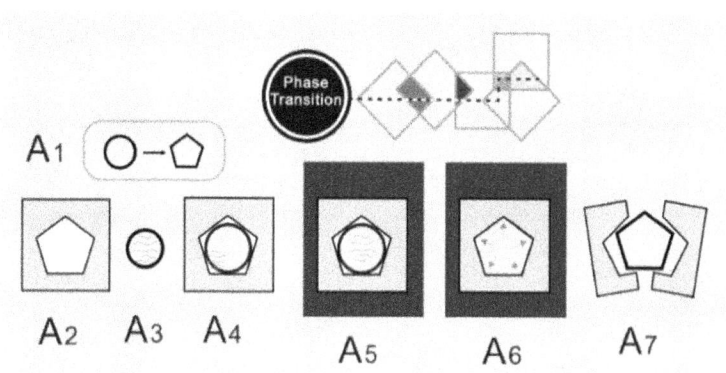

Phase Transition Can Be Applied Across Various Fields

A: Low-cost metal tube shaping method.
A1: The objective is to transform a round metal hollow tube into a pentagonal shape.
A2: Start by creating a pentagonal mold.
A3: Fill the circular metal hollow tube with water.
A4: Insert the round hollow tube into the pentagonal mold.
A5: Place it in the freezer.
A6: The water inside the circular hollow tube freezes, expanding in volume to twice its liquid state. The pressure from the ice expansion causes the round metal to conform to the pentagonal shape.
A7: Remove the mold to obtain a pentagonal metal hollow tube.

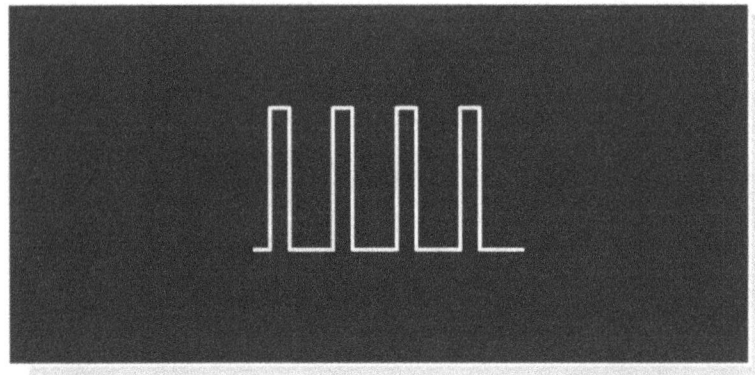

Periodic Action Can Be Executed Repeatedly

Periodic Action: Change the method of action from continuous to periodic or pulsating, achieving the desired results.

Specific operations:

1. Replace continuous action with Periodic Action or pulses.
2. If the action is already periodic, adjust its frequency.
3. Introduce pauses between pulses to enhance the action.

This is the 19th invention principle proposed by TRIZ that can solve problems.

LEO YUAN, PH.D.

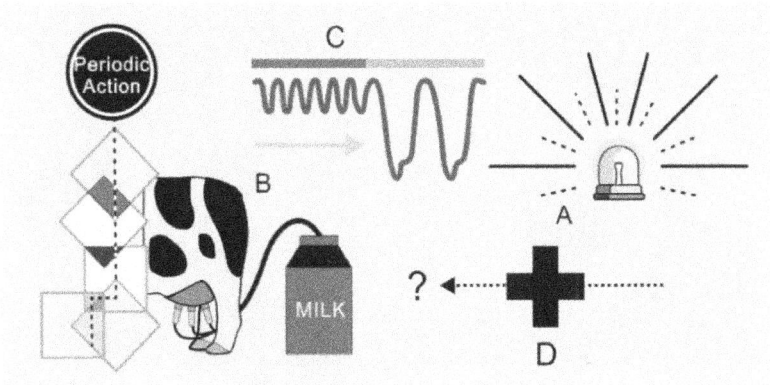

The Useful Periodic Action Can Warn and Save People

A: The warning light operates in a flashing manner, which is more eye-catching than continuously being on.

B: Cow and sheep milking machines.

C: Before the baby sucks breast milk, there is a fast sucking rhythm to help the mammary glands release milk; the next step is to gently and effectively extract the breast milk. If artificial breast pumps can be manufactured according to this rhythm, mothers will feel more comfortable and efficient.

D: Cardio Pulmonary Resuscitation (CPR).

Porous Materials Can Transmit Light and Block Large Particles

Porous Materials: Alter the state of gases, liquids, and solids to introduce porosity; that is, make the medium more porous by incorporating pores, bubbles, capillaries, etc., to serve one or more functions.

Specific operations:

1. Introduce porosity into objects or utilize objects with additional porous elements.

2. Pre-fill objects with materials if they have numerous holes.

This is the 31st invention principle proposed by TRIZ that can solve problems.

LEO YUAN, PH.D.

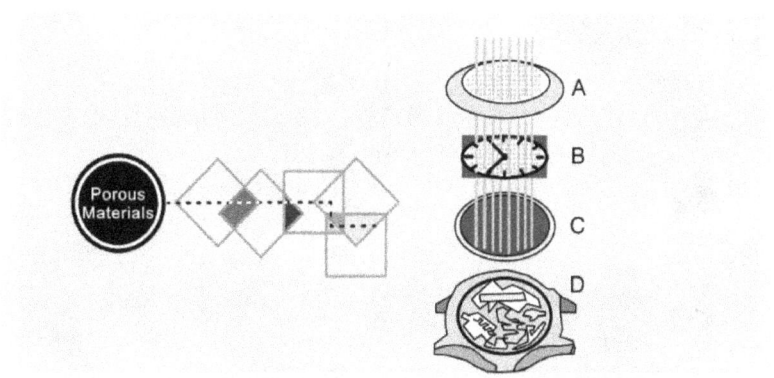

A Watch That Looks Good and Absorbs Solar Energy

A watch that can be charged by solar energy and is also aesthetically pleasing. Its structure includes:

A: Porous surface;
B: Porous watch face, which can feature attractive patterns;
C: Solar panel converts light into electricity;
D: Watch body.

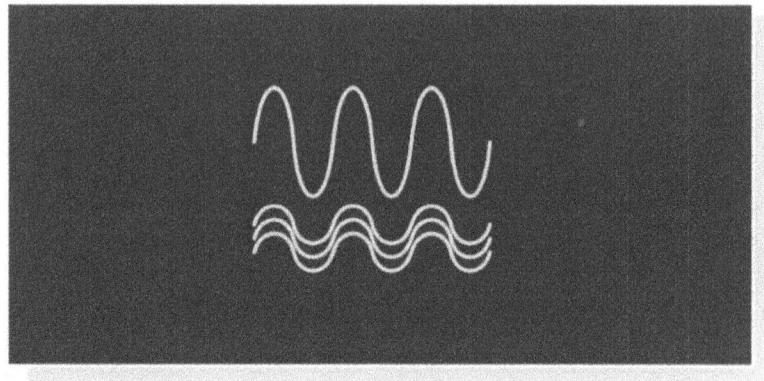

Mechanical Vibration Solves the Problem of Manual Inconvenience and Inaccuracy

Mechanical Vibration: Utilize vibration or periodic oscillation to achieve regular and periodic changes.
Specific operations:
1. Induce vibration in the object.
2. Utilize resonant frequencies.
3. Employ pressure vibration as an alternative to mechanical vibration.
4. Connect electromagnetic fields with ultrasonic vibrations.
5. If already vibrating, increase its frequency, possibly reaching ultrasonic waves.
This is the 18th invention principle proposed by TRIZ that can solve problems.

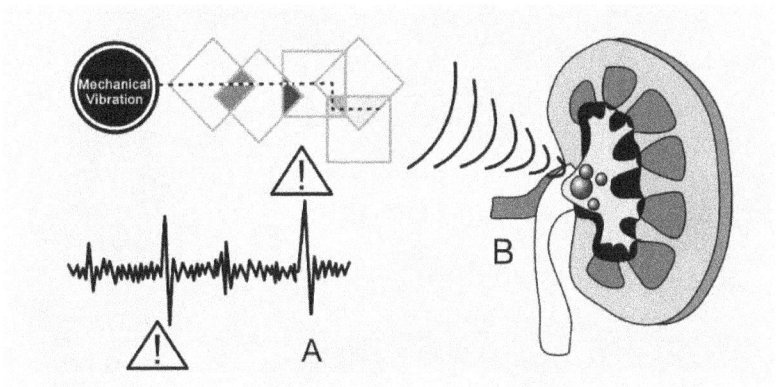

Simple Mechanical Vibration Solves Difficult Problems

A: Detecting the frequency of mechanical vibrations can identify abnormal frequencies and pinpoint the cause of faults early.

B: Using electric shock or an electromagnetic field to generate shock waves, focusing the energy through a precise positioning system to break kidney stones in the body.

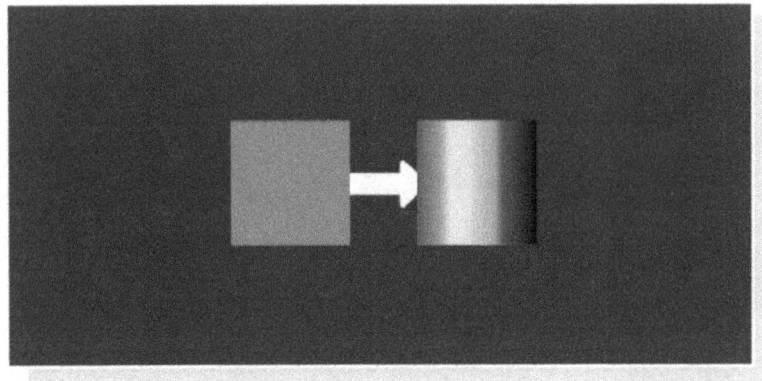

Transformation of Properties: Renovating to Achieve New Conditions

Transformation of Properties: Altering the properties within an object or system to create a more functional state.

Specific operations: Adjusting states, density, concentration, elasticity, temperature, and volume of objects.

This is the 35th invention principle proposed by TRIZ that can solve problems.

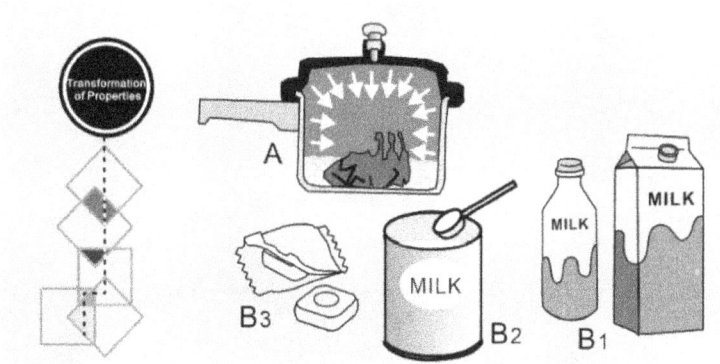

Transformation of Properties Can Enrich Our Lives

A: Pressure cooker: The higher pressure inside the pot, exceeding atmospheric pressure, increases the air pressure and temperature, cooking food faster.

B: Milk comes in three common forms: B1 liquid milk, B2 powdered milk, and B3 milk tablets.

Inert Environment: Effective Despite Its Low Effectiveness

Inert Environment: Create a neutral or inert atmosphere or environment to support the desired function.
Specific operations:
1. Replace the normal environment with an inert one.
2. Complete the operation process in a vacuum state.
3. Add neutral substances or additives to the object.
This is the 39th invention principle proposed by TRIZ that can solve problems.

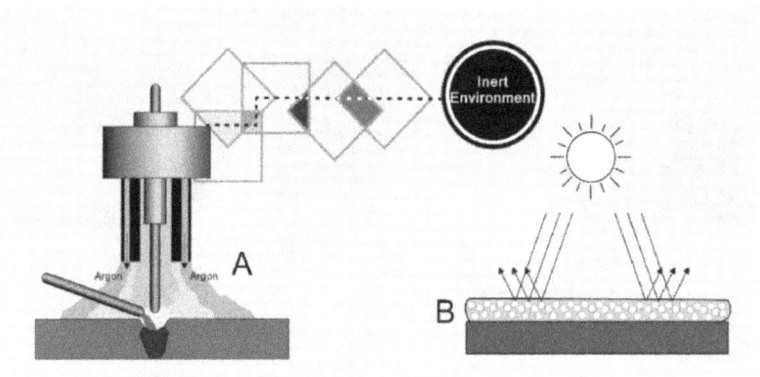

The Less Effective It Appears, The More Crucial It is for Functional Improvement

A: To prevent oxidation during welding, the welding arc's periphery is covered with argon inert gas.

B: Constant-temperature heat-insulating paint is composed of numerous small polymer-filled vacuum air pockets added to the paint. It features a lightweight texture and excellent heat insulation, forming a protective layer that is heat-insulating, sound-insulating, and waterproof.

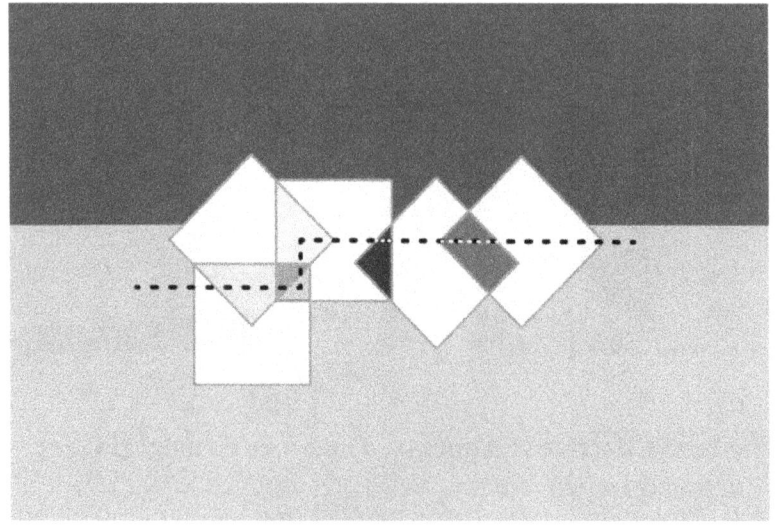

Invention Principles Cross-Border Association

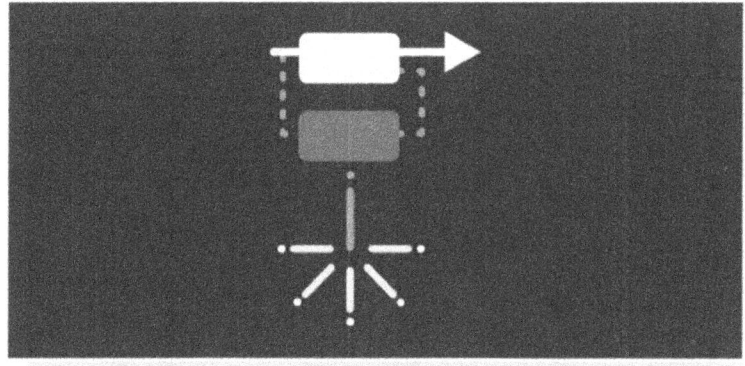

Feedback, A Principle Applicable Across Many Fields

Feedback: By returning the system's output as input, control over the output can be enhanced; in essence, any changes in the system or situation provide information that can be utilized to adjust actions.

Specific operations:

1. Implement feedback.
2. Reverse existing feedback if necessary.

This is the 23rd invention principle proposed by TRIZ that can solve problems.

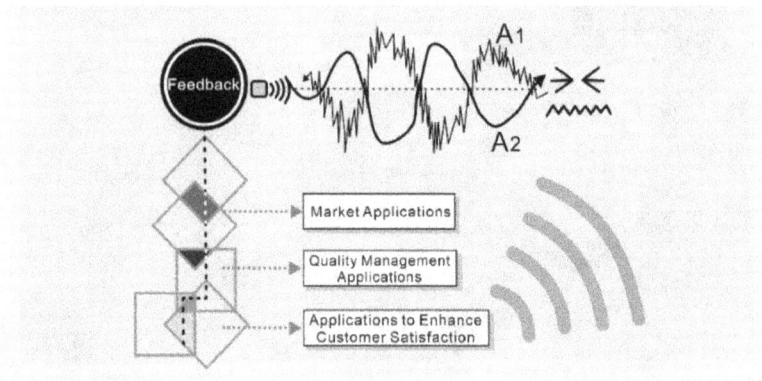

Feedback: Product Features and Market Applications

Anti-noise headphones utilize multiple microphones positioned close to the ears to capture external noise (A1). Electronic circuits (A2) then generate signals with a phase opposite to that of the noise wave. When this anti-phase signal is produced, it destructively interferes with and cancels out external noise.

Market Applications: Engage directly with designers and consumers.

Quality Management Applications: Implement systems for controlling non-conforming products, monitoring, and corrective actions.

Applications to Enhance Customer Satisfaction: 1.Offer new, non-profit services to encourage customers to provide feedback about their experiences.

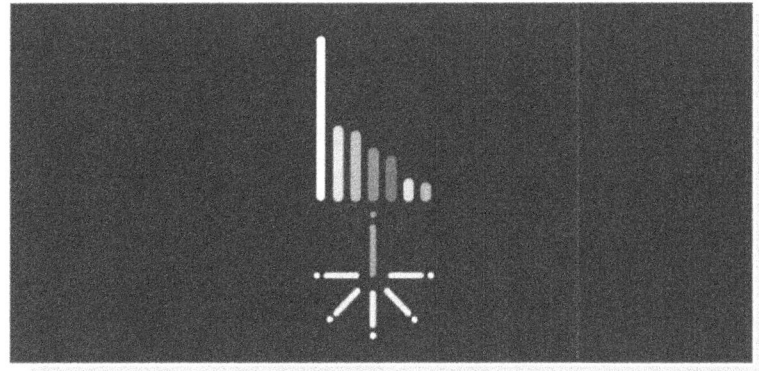

Partial or Excessive Action: Unbalanced Actions Are Sometimes Better

Partial or Excessive Action: Employing more actions or substances than necessary or using fewer actions or substances than required to address a problem.
Specific operations: If achieving 100% of the desired results is challenging, adjusting the quantity of actions or substances can significantly simplify the problem.
This is the 16th invention principle proposed by TRIZ that can solve problems.

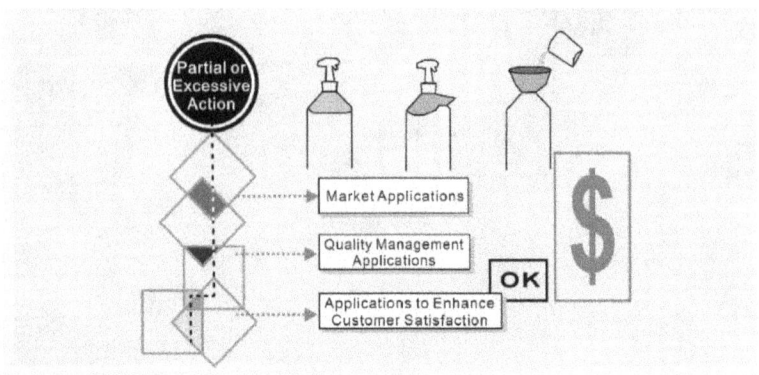

By Making Localized Changes to The Bottle Mouth, Its Functionality Can Be Enhanced

For instance, adding an extra silicone disc to the bottle mouth transforms it into a funnel when inverted, facilitating the addition of additional liquid.

Market Applications: Emphasizing minor advantages to enhance visual appeal.

Quality Management Applications: If a process is critical and high-risk, allocate additional resources to ensure its reliability and prevent frequent issues.

Applications to Enhance Customer Satisfaction: Avoid customer dissatisfaction by enhancing commitment and reducing return rates through additional service offerings as incentives.

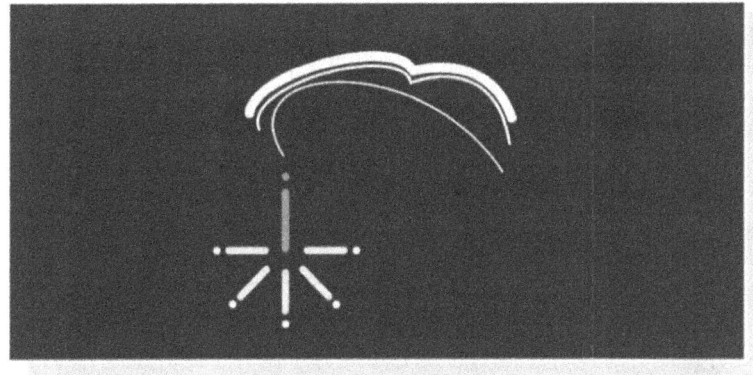

Flexible Shells and Thin Films: Harnessing Physical Phenomena for Great Utility

Flexible Shells and Thin Films: Utilize membranes to substitute traditional components, or employ membranes or elastic films to isolate an object or its surroundings.

Specific Operations:

1. Replace the original structure with elastic films and membranes.

2. Use a thin film to effectively isolate the object from its external environment.

This principle, the 30th proposed by TRIZ, offers effective solutions to various problems.

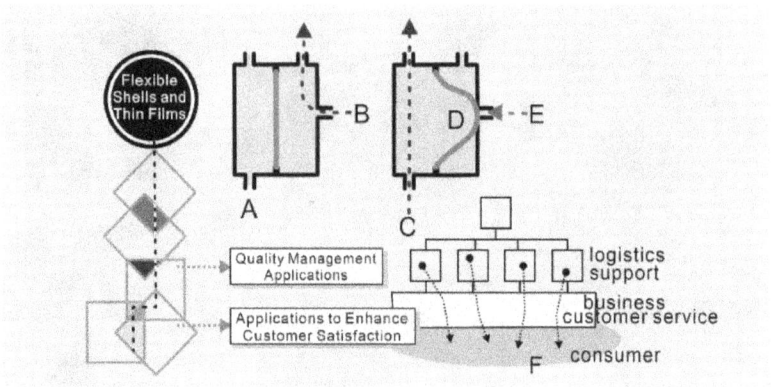

**Without Special Filling, Other Gases Can Pass Through.
With Special Filling, Other Gases Are Blocked**

A: No airflow passes through; the film remains stationary. B: Airflow can pass through. C: Airflow passes through, generating pressure. D: The film expands and presses against another airflow inlet. E: The film is pressed, preventing airflow entry.

Quality Management Applications: Implementing a flat organizational structure or network communication, reducing hierarchy between senior executives and customers.

Applications to Enhance Customer Satisfaction: Rotating business and customer service departments to increase frontline opportunities for customer interaction.

Segmentation Can Concentrate or Disperse Resources

Segmentation: Dividing a system into parts or isolating/integrating specific system properties, whether harmful or useful.
Specific operations:
1. Divide the object into independent parts.
2. Integrate parts into a combined object.
3. Increase the level of object segmentation.
This is the first inventive principle proposed by TRIZ for problem-solving.

Advancing the Medici Fusion

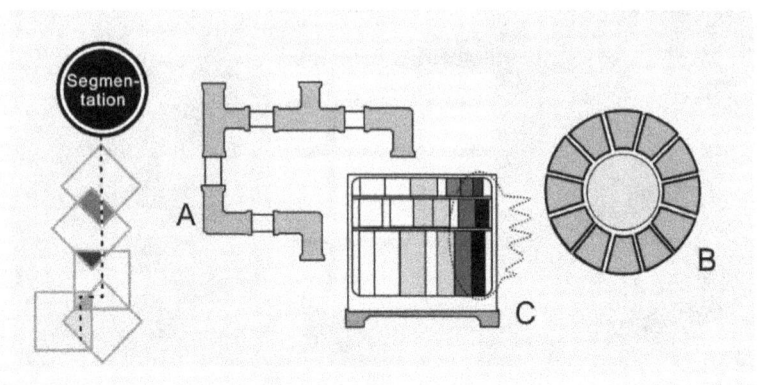

It's Easy to Overheat or Puncture, Especially in Small Spaces

A: By dividing water pipes into several standardized components, costs can be reduced.

B: Dividing the tire into several independent parts allows it to continue traveling for a certain distance even if punctured by sharp objects.

C: The host's parts are divided into four "temperature isolation zones" with independent temperature control. Each zone has its own dedicated low-speed fan, significantly reducing overall noise. This solves the problem of needing to increase fan speed to lower temperature, which typically generates excessive noise.

LEO YUAN, PH.D.

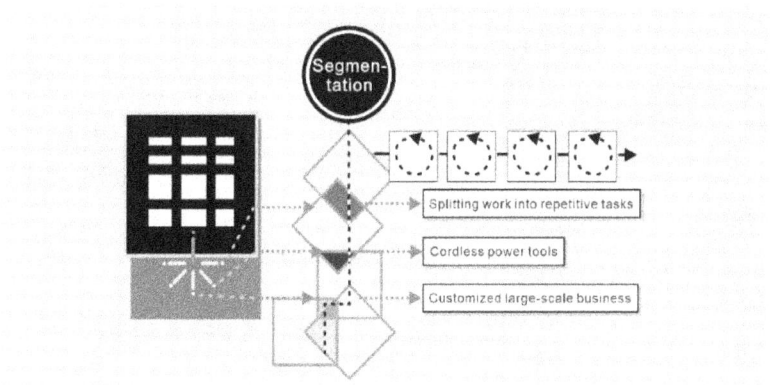

Extended Thinking on Segmentation: The Wider the Association, The More Creativity There Will Be

By applying the idea of segmentation to the actual market, many ideas can be generated, such as: 1. Decomposing a large restaurant into a series of smaller, comfortable, home-like restaurants, and connecting them all together. 2. Breaking down a project into smaller parts can help control the project's delivery dates and improve overall execution.

Quality Management Applications: Scientific management involves dividing work into repetitive and simple tasks.

Applications to Enhance Customer Satisfaction: Large-scale customization treats every customer as a unique market segment.

Extraction: Working Independently or Removing Inefficient Parts

Extraction involves separating harmful or useful components and properties from the entire system, then identifying the unique characteristics of the system after separation.

Specific Operations:

1. Extract, remove, and separate undesirable parts or attributes from an object.
2. Extract only the necessary parts or attributes and discard the rest.

This is the second invention principle proposed by TRIZ that can solve problems.

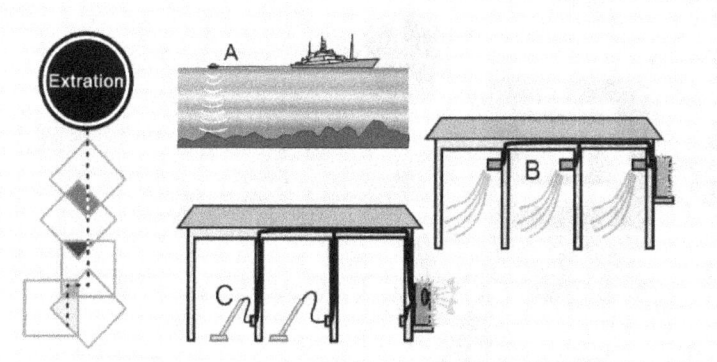

Extraction: Can Be Processed Separately or Centrally

A: If a sonar detector that detects fish schools and the depth of seabed terrain is placed in the center of the ship, it will easily vibrate due to the engine and lose detection accuracy. Use a extraction method to position the sonar detector 100 meters away from the ship so that it can detect accurately.

B: The compressor in a split air conditioner is placed outside to isolate the noise.

C: In a standalone vacuum cleaner, the exhaust motor is positioned outside, resulting in a completely silent indoor vacuum cleaner.

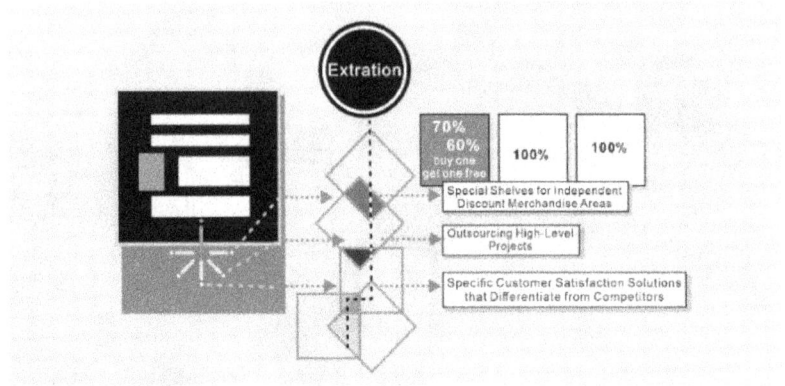

Extraction Applications: Outsourcing Transactions

Extraction practices are prevalent in various fields: 1. They impact both product manufacturing processes and commercial sales processes by separating components that cause conflicts and outsourcing them to external manufacturers for processing. 2. Distance teaching or remote work are prime examples of extraction methods.

Applications to Enhance Customer Satisfaction:
1. Implementing dedicated shelves and a specific discount product area. 2. Differentiating from competitors by developing promotional programs tailored to satisfy specific customers.

Quality Management Applications: Outsourcing high-level professional tasks to external vendors.

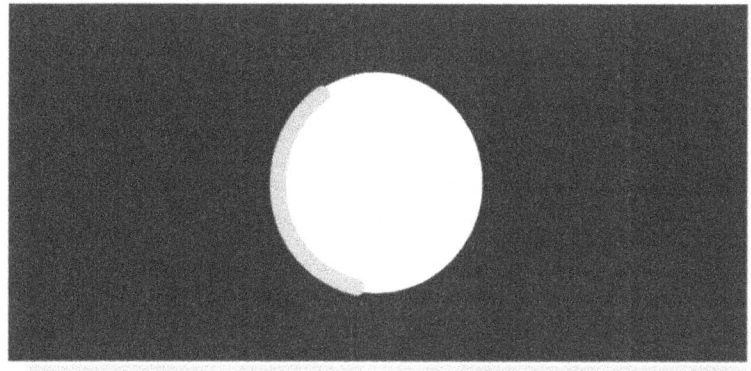

Local Quality: Strengthen Optimization of Specific Areas

Local Quality: Modify the characteristics of an item in a specific area to achieve the desired functionality or to optimize specific resources.
Specific Operations:
1. Transform an object composed of identical components into a structure made of different components.
2. Utilize objects with varying parts to achieve different functions.
3. Place each part of the object in the most suitable condition for its operation. This is the third invention principle proposed by TRIZ that can solve problems.

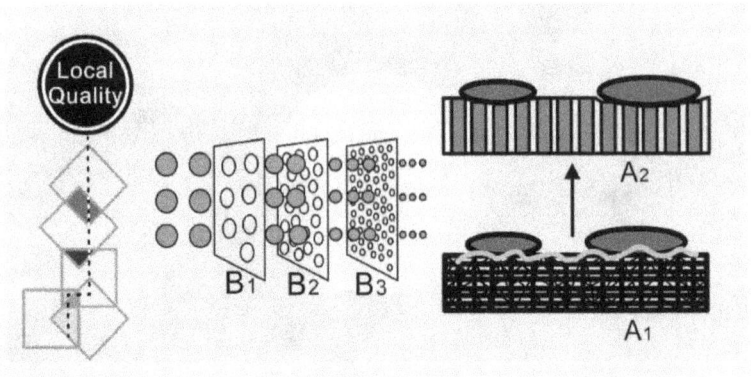

Improving Local Problems Individually to Solve the Overall Issue

A: A1: Traditional connected spring bed—Each spring is linked in series with steel wires to form a spring network, with reinforced edges using steel bars. A2: Independent cylinder spring mattress—Each spring is individually wrapped in a long non-woven bag and fixed with hot melt glue or a staple gun. This design allows for individual springs to be adjusted or turned without affecting the adjacent springs.

B: If a single filter is used, it can quickly become blocked by large particles, reducing its effectiveness and shortening its lifespan. By dividing the filtration process into: B1: Filtering large particles, B2: Filtering small particles, and B3: Filtering extremely small particles, the efficiency and longevity of the filtration system can be improved.

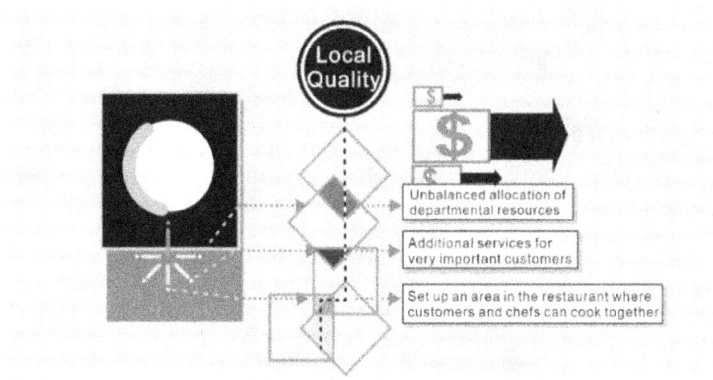

Local Quality Application: Smoothing Operations in Small Areas

1. Chain restaurants launch localized meals through franchises and enhance promotions. 2. Plan workplaces based on employee psychology and ergonomics to increase employee retention.

Quality Management Applications: Address unbalanced departmental resource allocation.

Market Applications: Establish restaurant areas where customers can cook together with chefs.

Applications to Enhance Customer Satisfaction: Offer bonuses, discounts, or additional services to your most valuable customers.

Asymmetry, there may be effects that symmetry cannot achieve

Asymmetry: Transform from having symmetrical properties to non-symmetrical properties.
Specific operations:
1. Replace symmetrically shaped objects with asymmetrically shaped objects.
2. If an object is already asymmetrical, increase its degree of asymmetry.
This is the fourth invention principle proposed by TRIZ that can solve problems.

LEO YUAN, PH.D.

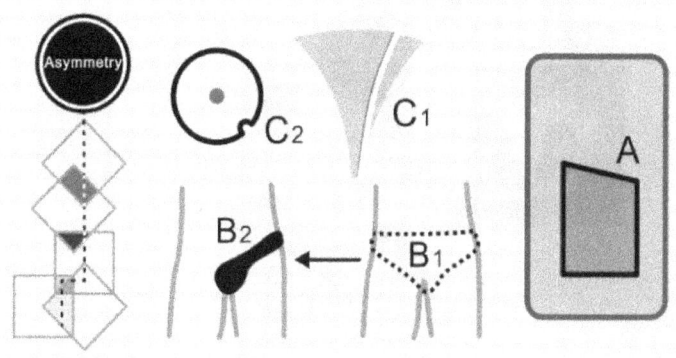

With Asymmetry's design, the world is more convenient and exciting

A: Designing an asymmetrically shaped mobile phone battery can resolve issues related to the correct installation orientation of positive and negative poles during replacement.

B: Men's summer underwear options include B1, traditional underwear, and B2, which covers and connects at only one end, adding a touch of allure.

C: Adding grooves to the curved sides of a funnel can increase the flow rate by up to 300% compared to traditional funnels, allowing liquids to pass through instantly.

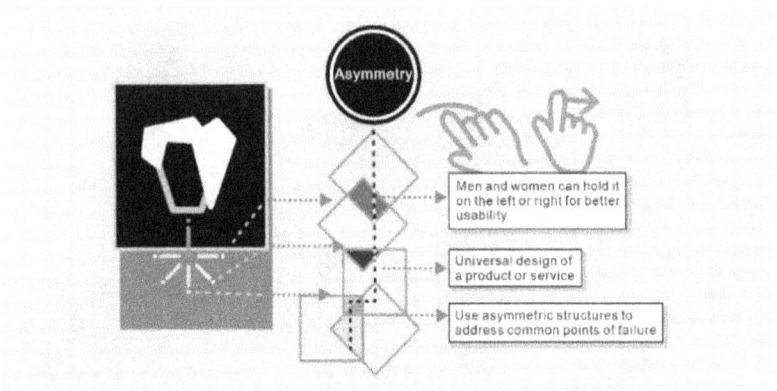

Asymmetry Applications Can Sometimes Be More Thoughtful

1. Use asymmetrical presentation methods to design web pages that capture customers' attention. 2. The asymmetrically shaped desk can be adjusted to suit the work characteristics of each department, meeting the work needs and ensuring comfort for each employee.

Applications to Enhance Customer Satisfaction:
1. Unisex design allows both men and women to hold the product on the left or right, making asymmetric designs easier to use.
2. Implement universal design across products or services, ensuring applicability to diverse groups.

Quality Management Applications: Implement an asymmetric structure to address the root causes of frequent failures.

LEO YUAN, PH.D.

Merging: Integration into a Unified Whole and Removal of Redundancies

Merging involves reintegrating the functions, features, and components of a system to create new, satisfying, or unique attributes. This process entails adding new substances or technologies into an existing system to enhance its performance and functionality. It involves connecting or combining similar or related objects, tasks, or functional entities that require consecutive operations.

Specific operations: 1. Combine homogeneous objects or objects that involve continuous operations in space. 2. Merge homogeneous or continuous operations in time.

This is the fifth invention principle proposed by TRIZ to solve problems.

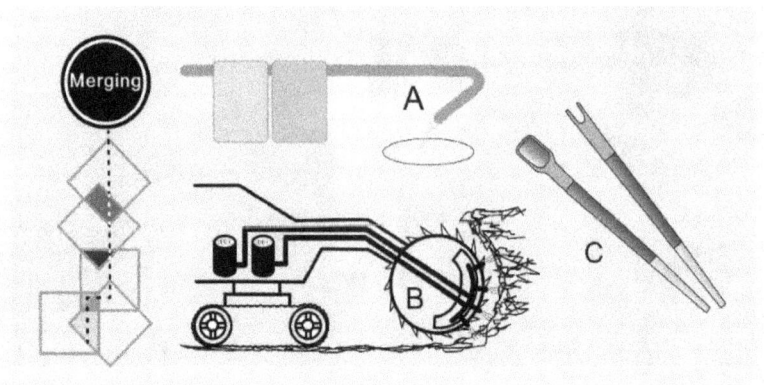

Merging's Design Can Be Very Fashionable and Modern

A: The water pipe, faucet, and towel rail are integrated into one, creating a simple and multipurpose design.

B: Rotate the excavator, boil hot water in the car, and use water pipes to transport it to the front. Use special steam nozzles to melt and soften the frozen land. At this time, the circular saw rotates to move the melted snow, allowing for faster progress.

C: Combine chopsticks with spoons and forks.

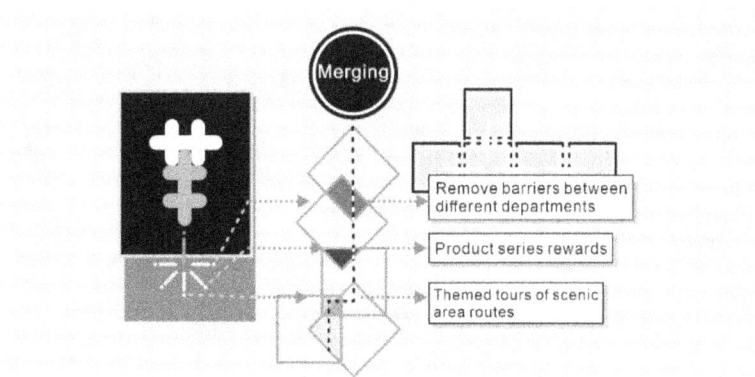

Merging Application is a Simple and Convenient Method

1. Select the best local snacks and host a snack banquet in a large restaurant.
2. Install optical fiber network cables in existing water pipes to eliminate urban ground construction and save space.

Quality Management Applications: Remove barriers between different departments.

Applications to Enhance Customer Satisfaction:
1. Scenic area themed route guide for one-stop sightseeing.
2. Implement incentive promotions for each series of branded products, such as movie hero series and sports team series.

Universality: No Matter How You Operate It, It Can Do Anything

Universality: Make the system more consistent and all-encompassing. This involves using the same object, action, or feature for different purposes or in different ways.

Specific operations: Create multifunctional objects that eliminate the need for other objects.

This is the sixth invention principle proposed by TRIZ that can solve problems.

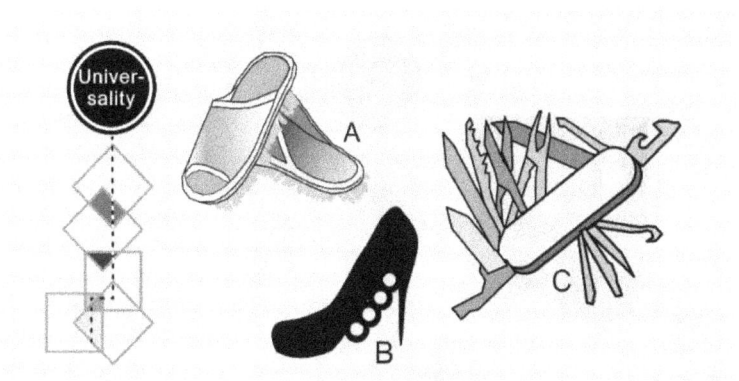

A Swiss Army Knives, Capable of Performing Hundreds of Operations

A: The bottom of the slippers is made of fluffy towel strips that mop the floor while walking.

B: There are Brass Knuckles on the bottom of the high heels, which can be used as a self-defense weapon when needed.

C: A Swiss Army Knives has 115 uses, including combinations such as saws, pliers, bottle openers, and knives.

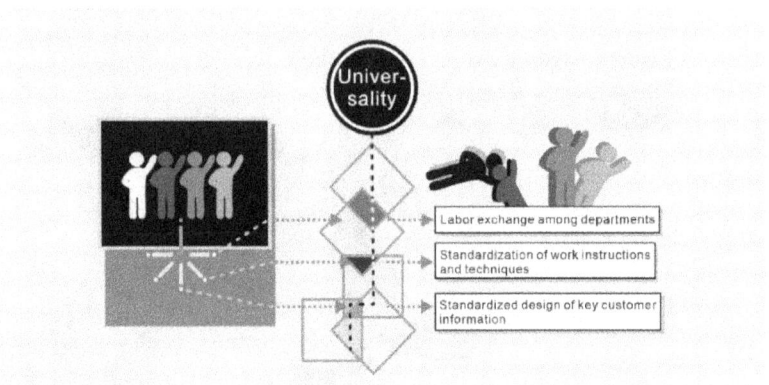

Universality Applications Can Be More Comprehensive

1. Hire multi-skilled workers who possess both technical and business marketing skills. 2. A multi-purpose van that accommodates multiple people, provides sleeping space, and carries cargo.
Quality Management Applications:
1. Labor exchange among various departments.
2. Standardization of work instructions and techniques.
Applications to Enhance Customer Satisfaction: Standardized design of key customer-related information, such as user manuals, warranties, complaint forms, satisfaction feedback, etc.

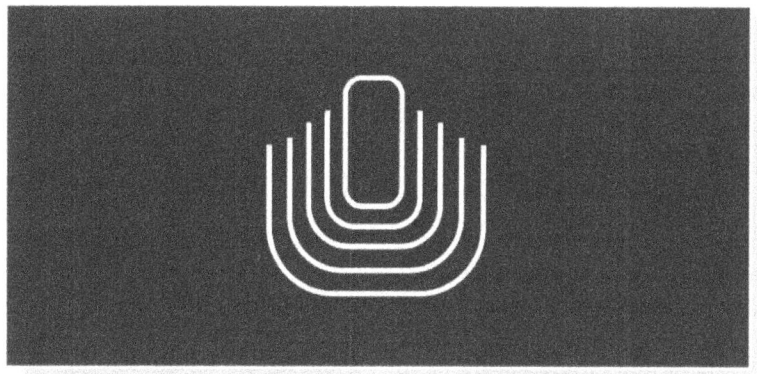

Nesting: Efficiently Storing Multiple Items in a Compact Space

Nesting utilizes a structure that allows systems or components to closely integrate with each other. This involves integrating objects with different functions into a single system, resulting in a system with diverse and complementary properties.

Specific operations:

1. Objects can be sequentially placed inside another object.
2. An object can pass through the hole of another object.

This is the seventh invention principle proposed by TRIZ, capable of solving various problems.

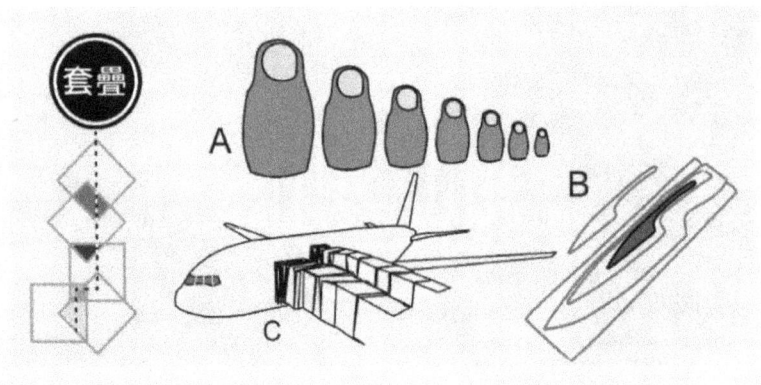

Nesting: Flexible and Extendable, Efficient Storage in Compact Form

A: Russian dolls. Each doll contains a smaller doll within it, allowing several dolls to be nested inside each other.

B: Knife set. Knives are stacked continuously, with each layer capable of holding multiple knives.

C: Jet bridge, also known as a boarding bridge or jetway, transforms the walkway leading to an aircraft into a telescopic structure. This design saves space occupied by traditional connecting doors and offers adjustable length flexibility.

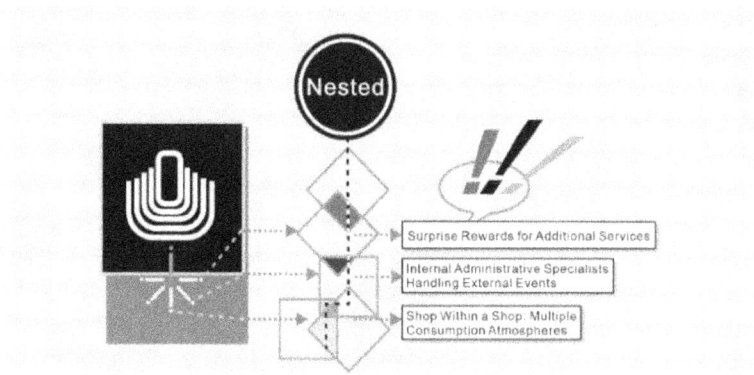

Nested Applications: Unveiling Constant Surprises

1. Profit centers within organizational structures or employee intrapreneurship initiatives resemble "companies within a company," fostering activities nested within broader activities. 2. Project processes can benefit from initial quality inspections on smaller components before comprehensive assessments are conducted.

Applications to Enhance Customer Satisfaction:
1. Surprise customers with additional service rewards.
2. Store-within-a-store concepts create diverse consumption environments within a single location.

Quality Management Applications: Assign traditional internal affairs employees to handle external events.

Prior Counteraction: Preventing Errors Before They Occur

Prior Counteraction: Take action in advance to eliminate, reduce, or prevent errors where they may occur. In other words, using Prior Counteraction allows for the elimination, reduction, or prevention of undesired functions, events, or conditions in the future.

Specific operations:

1. Consider the reaction force in advance if necessary.
2. Apply counter-tension preemptively if an object requires tension.

This is the ninth invention principle proposed by TRIZ that can solve problems.

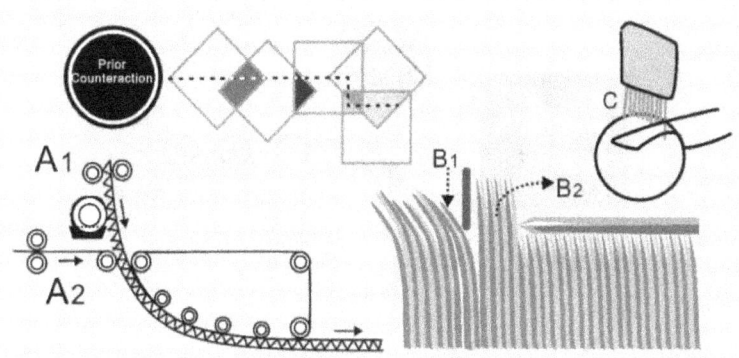

Trim the grass to a lower height initially, allowing it to rebound just enough to be cut neatly

A: Production of Corrugated Fiberboard. A1: The upper half of the paper is transported. A2: Glue is applied to the round roller. As the paper moves, it picks up the glue and adheres to the lower half.

B: Lawn Mower. B1: Deliberately place a plastic partition in front of the circular knife. When the lawn mower moves forward, the plastic partition pushes the grass ahead. B2: After the lawn mower moves forward, the suppressed grass rebounds. As it rebounds, it reaches the optimal height to be neatly cut by the circular saw.

C: Fruit Slicing Tool. Use a comb-like shaping tool to press round fruits, ensuring they are uniformly sliced with ease.

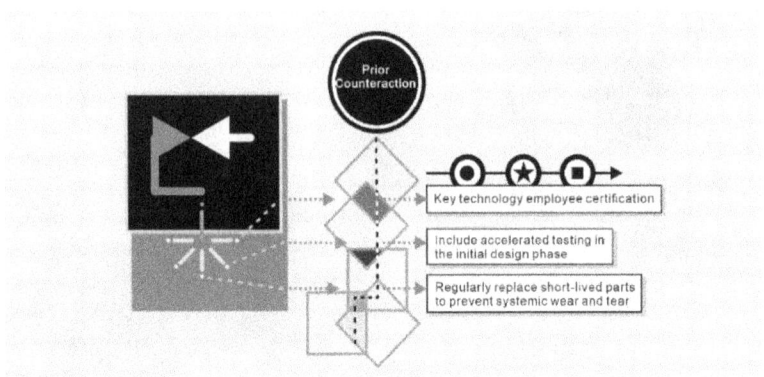

Prior Counteraction Application: Taking Proactive Steps in Advance

1. Prior to engaging in high-risk activities, announce potential negative impacts. 2. When conducting customer surveys, inquire about customers' least preferred features in new products.
Quality Management Applications:
1. Essential technologies require advance employee certification.
2. Regularly replace short-life parts to prevent systemic wear and tear.
Applications to Enhance Customer Satisfaction: Implement accelerated or stress testing in the initial stages to preemptively address potential failure areas, such as aging, voltage stress, and thermal shock.

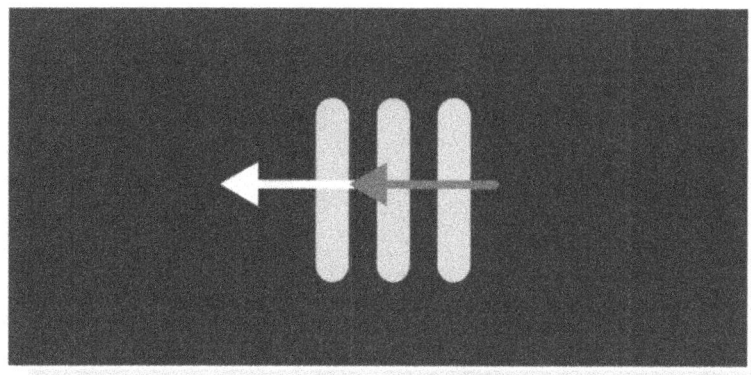

Prior Action: Completing Part of the Work in Advance

Prior Action involves taking steps before an incident occurs to enhance efficiency, safety, and operational ease, thereby gaining advantages. Specific operations:
1. Complete all actions beforehand, or at least some critical ones.
2. Position objects for immediate action, minimizing waiting time.

This is the 10th invention principle proposed by TRIZ to solve problems.

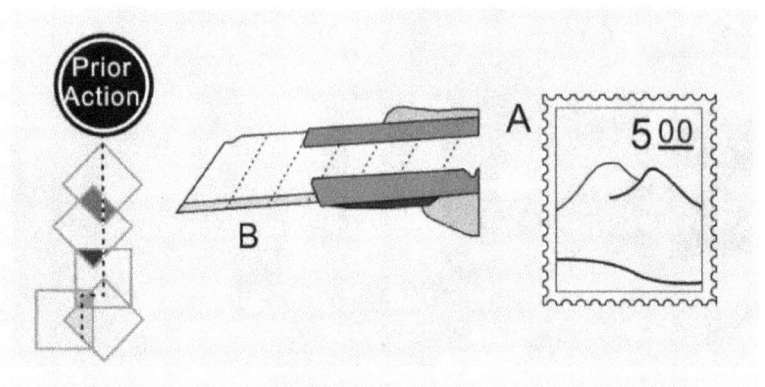

If You Finish the First Half First, It Will Be Much Easier for the Next Person to Take Over

A: Drill perforated holes around the stamp to make it easier for the user to tear the stamp apart.

B: Create grooves on the utility blade to facilitate breaking the dull part of the blade and restoring sharpness.

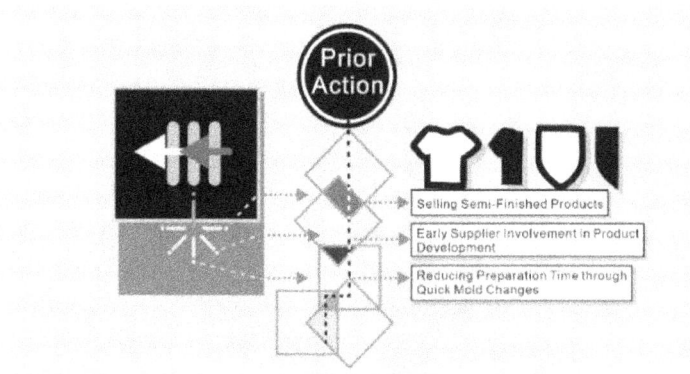

Prior Action Application to Expedite Work

1. Product development engineers must first work in sales and service before engaging in product development. 2. Begin by creating preliminary activities to demonstrate the value of the new product to potential customers, followed by launching promotional activities for the new product.

Applications to Enhance Customer Satisfaction:
1. Offer semi-finished products for sale. 2. Initiate advertising during the product and service research and development stage, such as fundraising for product development.

Quality Management Applications: 1. Implement rapid mold change methods to reduce preparation time. 2. Involve suppliers in the early stages of product design (ESI, Early Supplier Involvement).

Inversion: Sometimes You Want to Invert, and That's Right

Inversion: Acting in the opposite way, turning the inside into the outside, and reversing the top to the bottom; in other words, thinking in reverse.
Specific operations: 1. Perform actions in the opposite direction instead of following conventional actions. 2. Fix and immobilize the movable parts of an object or the external environment, and invert the object upside down.
This is the 13th invention principle proposed by TRIZ that can solve problems.

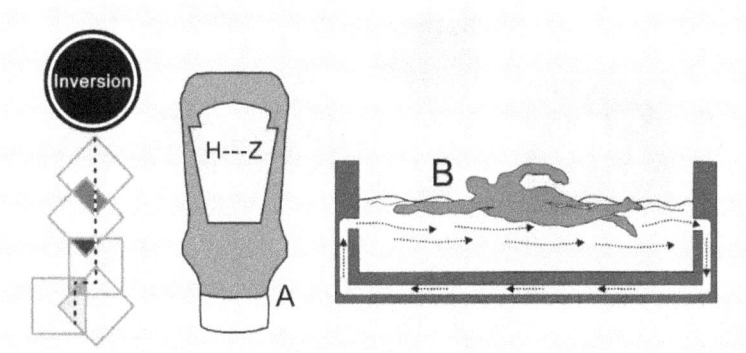

It May Be Better to Reverse the Direction of Action

A: Invert the bottle so that the opening faces downward, allowing viscous tomato sauce to pour out easily.

B: Keep people stationary while moving water, allowing swimmers to train in a confined space. This concept is akin to a treadmill: the conveyor belt moves backward, causing the user to move forward while running, creating the illusion of running in place.

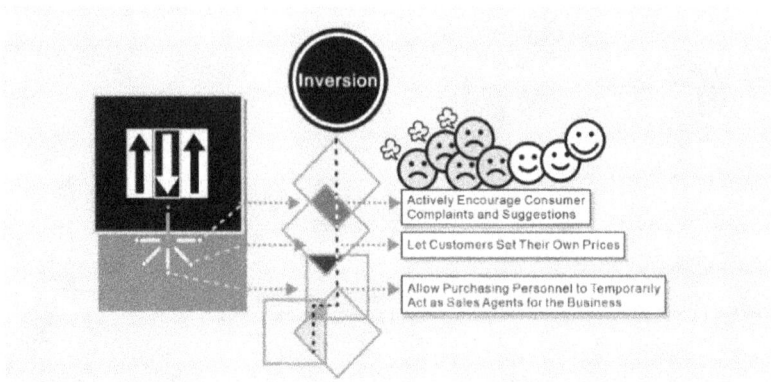

Inversion Application: Engaging the Other Party

The mobile library delivers books to your doorstep, while the mobile book return box allows you to simply scan the barcode, drop the books in, and return them.

Quality Management Applications:
1. Actively encourage consumer complaints and suggestions. 2. Use provocative techniques in free discussion sessions to flip issues upside down and stir up argumentative emotions to generate more ideas.

Applications to Enhance Customer Satisfaction:
1. Allow purchasing staff to temporarily act as business sales agents, and vice versa. 2. Let customers set their own prices. Create new topics and events to capture everyone's attention.

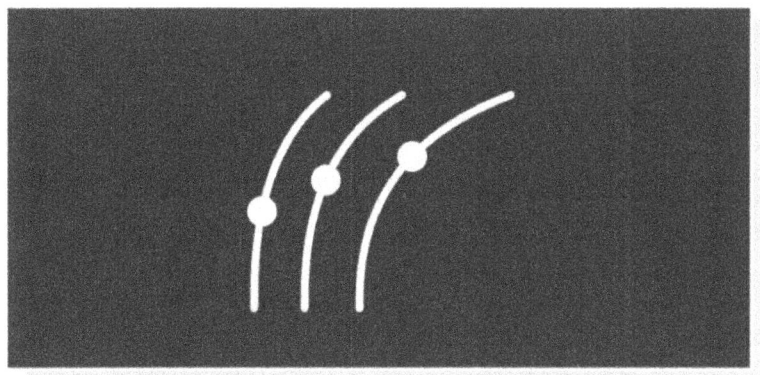

Dynamics Makes Things More Flexible and Allows Them to Be Moved at Any Time

Dynamics: Making a system, state, or characteristic ephemeral, temporary, movable, adjustable, elastic, or changeable.

Specific operations: 1. Enable the characteristics of the object or the external environment to automatically adjust to achieve optimal performance at each stage of operation. 2. Divide the object into elements so that the position between each element can be changed. Make an immovable object movable. This is the 15th invention principle proposed by TRIZ that can solve problems.

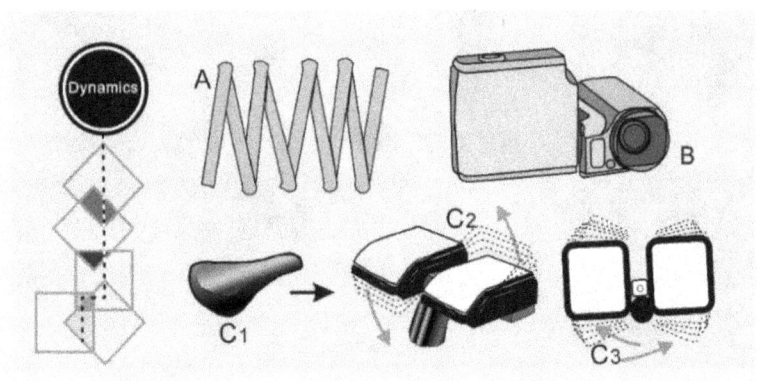

Build the Structure of Dynamics to Make the Product Easier to Use

A: Design the camera lens to be dynamic and rotatable to increase shooting flexibility.

B: The ruler is segmented into parts that can change their relative positions, and the folding design facilitates storage.

C: C1: The traditional bicycle seat is too small and uncomfortable to sit on; C2: Design a new type of seat cushion that comfortably accommodates the buttocks with dual cushions, allowing movement up and down along with the movement of the buttocks and thighs; C3: It can also move from side to side.

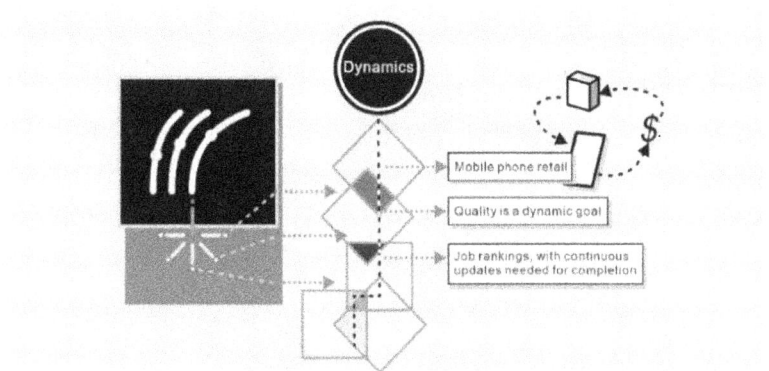

Dynamics Application, Broader Development Direction

1. Maintain organizational system planning for employees' continuous learning. 2. Mobile factory concept. 3. The flashlight features a gooseneck-shaped tube that can dynamically adjust the lighting direction.
Market Applications: Mobile phone retail.
Quality Management Applications:
1. Quality is an evolving goal.
2. Work ranking list with continuous updates needed for completion.

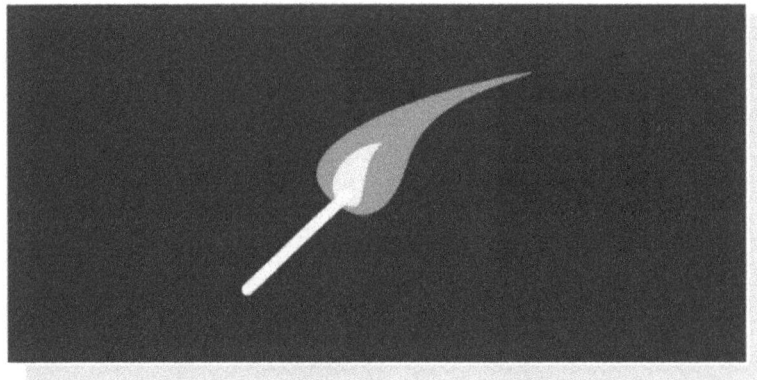

Accelerated Oxidation: Accelerating the transformation or performance of a substance

Accelerated Oxidation: Utilizing oxidation to enhance the efficiency of a function or process; in other words, using oxidants to increase the value within a system.

Specific operations: 1. Substitute ordinary air with enriched air. 2. Replace enriched air with oxygen. 3. Ionize within air or oxygen. 4. Utilize oxygen ions.

This is the 38th invention principle proposed by TRIZ that can solve problems.

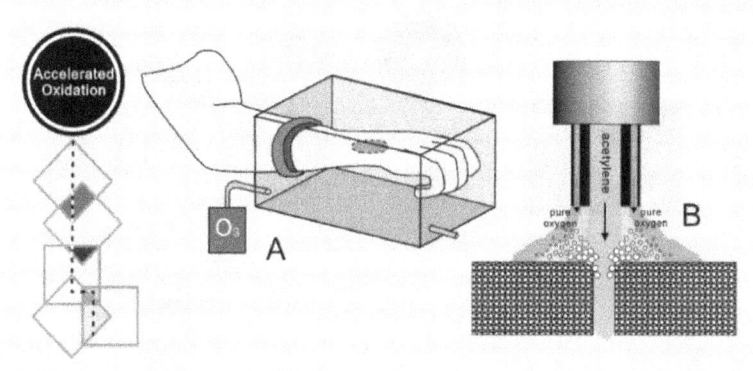

Remove Harmful Substances and Use Oxidation Effect to Solve Problems

A: Injecting ozone directly into a closed box can accelerate the treatment of wounds or skin diseases.

B: When cutting steel plates with acetylene, sparks from steel fines are easily produced. Adding pure oxygen around the acetylene accelerates the oxidation of the fines, effectively burning them directly. This modification creates a steel plate cutter that does not produce sparks.

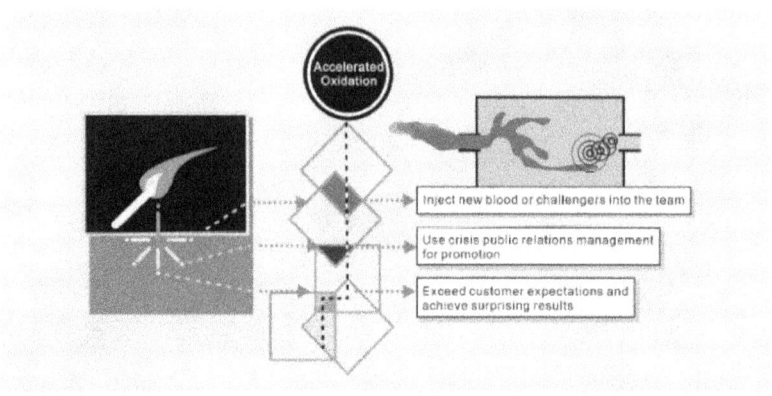

Accelerated Oxidation Applied to Other Fields

1. The restaurant's open kitchen adopts a customer-specified ordering mode.
2. Use simulation and gaming methods for teaching. 3. Use visual exhibitions for employee training.

Quality Management Applications: Inject new blood or challengers into the team.

Market Applications: Utilize crisis public relations for promotion.

Applications to Enhance Customer Satisfaction: Exceed customer expectations to surprise them and gain an advantage over competitors.

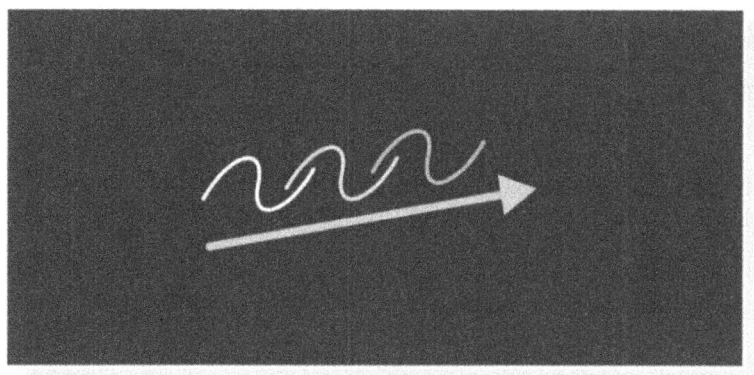

Continuity of Useful Action: Operating, Repairing, and Maintaining Simultaneously

Continuity of Useful Action: Establishing continuous action or eliminating all stagnant, indirect movement to increase efficiency.

Specific operations:

1. Complete an action without interruption, with all parts of an object remaining fully engaged.
2. Remove idle and intermediate parts.
3. Alter the reciprocating motion's direction.

This is the 20th invention principle proposed by TRIZ that can solve problems.

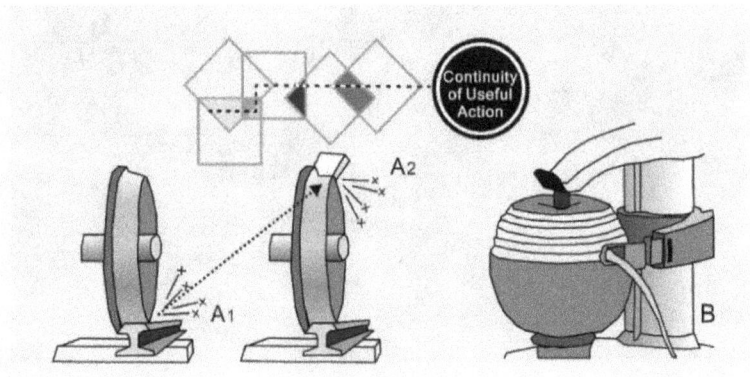

Continuity of Useful Action: Movement as Maintenance, Constant Rotation as Cutting

A: During the rotation of train wheels, A1 they often wear and deform. Use A2 special cutting tools to repair and maintain the specified shape at any time, ensuring they fit the rail shape and avoiding the need to disassemble the wheels for adjustment.

B: In a peeling machine, fix the round fruit securely. The peeler conforms to the surface of the fruit and can rotate to peel off the skin.

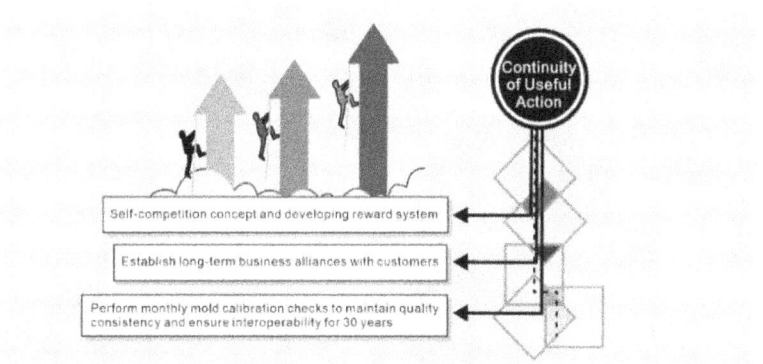

Connect Every Part Closely So That It Can Be Carried Out Continuously
Quality Management Applications:

1. Strengthen the concept of self-competition and develop relevant reward systems. 2. Conduct monthly mold calibration inspections to maintain consistent quality, ensuring product parts remain interoperable even after 30 years.

Applications to Enhance Customer Satisfaction:

1. Establish long-term business alliances with customers. 2. Maintain the consistent image in customers' minds and establish customer standards based on cooperative practices. 3. Provide 24-hour car service. Operators will pick up the car at night for maintenance and return it by breakfast time the next day.

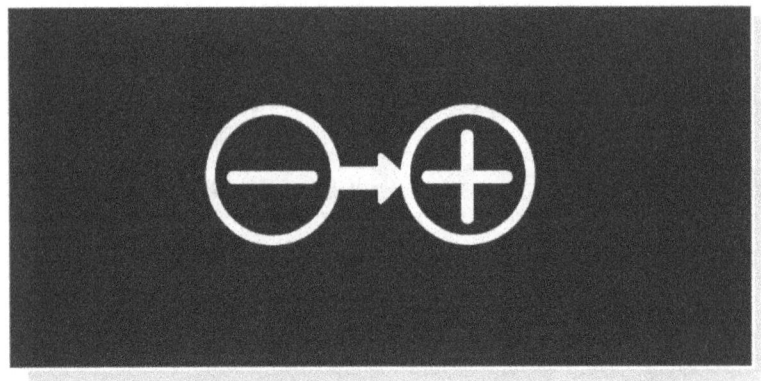

Convert Harm into Benefit, From Negative to Positive, or from Negative to Positive

Convert Harm into Benefit: Transform existing harmful factors into advantageous ones by altering material properties or enhancing value. Specific operations:
1. Utilize harmful environmental factors to achieve a positive effect.
2. Introduce another harmful factor to neutralize the original one.
3. Increase the intensity of harmful actions until they cease causing damage.
This is the 22nd invention principle proposed by TRIZ that can solve problems.

LEO YUAN, PH.D.

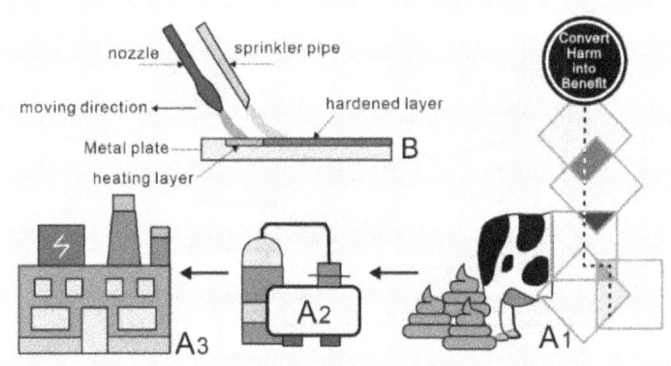

Every Substance Has Specific Physical Properties and is Useful When Used in the Right Place

A: Biogas power generation utilizes biogas from A1 animal excrement and garbage dumps as fuel. It is stored in the A2 biogas tank and transported to the A3 power plant. After combustion, it generates steam heat to drive the turbine and generate electricity.

B: When heating metal with high-frequency current, only the outer layer is heated. This phenomenon is utilized for surface heat treatment.

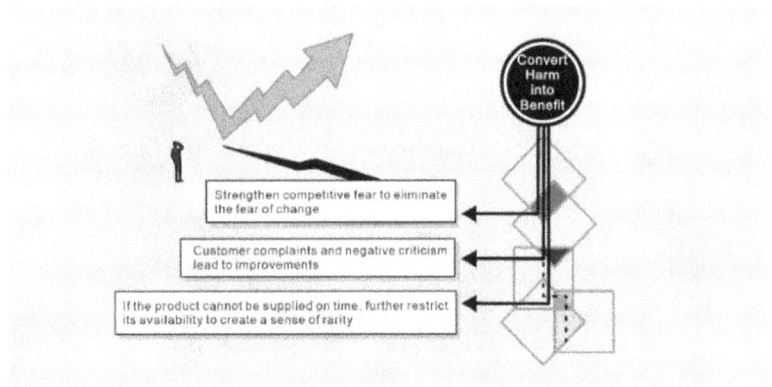

Convert Harm into Benefit: Approach Situations with a Positive Attitude
Quality Management Applications:

1. Embrace competition fears to eradicate the fear of change.
2. Utilize customer complaints and negative feedback as opportunities for improvement.

Market Applications:

1. If goods cannot be supplied on time, adjust the strategy by further limiting the supply quantity to create a sense of rarity and value.
2. Surprising customers who have experienced your product or service can enhance their impression, often surpassing scenarios without any issues.

LEO YUAN, PH.D.

Dispose, makes it easier for us to do things

Dispose: Utilize cheaper, simpler, or easier-to-handle objects to reduce costs, enhance convenience, and extend lifespan.

Specific operation: Replace expensive objects with accumulated inexpensive alternatives.

This is the 27th invention principle proposed by TRIZ, which aims to solve problems effectively.

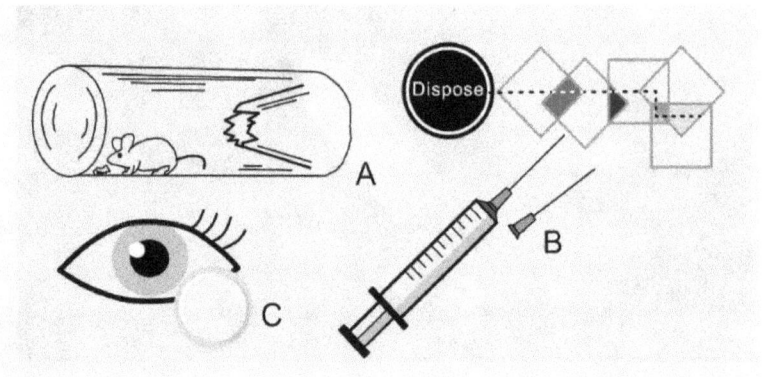

The Dispose Design is Very Convenient. It Would Be Better If It Were Environmentally Friendly

A: The plastic tube of the disposable mousetrap bait. When the mouse enters the trap through the conical opening, the spiked end prevents the mouse from escaping.

B: Disposable needles are simply discarded after use. Other examples include disposable diapers, paper pants, lightweight raincoats, masks, and other disposable products.

C: Disposable contact lenses.

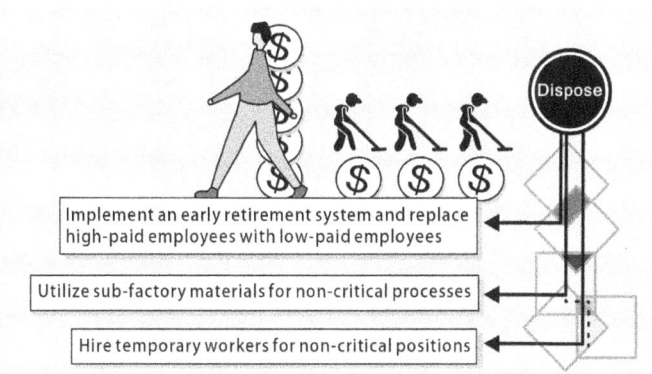

Dispose Application Allows for More Flexible Scheduling

Personnel Management Applications: Establish an early retirement system and replace high-paid old employees with low-paid employees. A key strategy is to hire retired old employees as consultants at relatively lower salaries.

Quality Management Applications:
For non-critical positions, hire temporary employees or part-time workers paid by the hour.
For parts or materials in non-critical processes, use sub-factories instead of expensive parts or materials from the main factory.

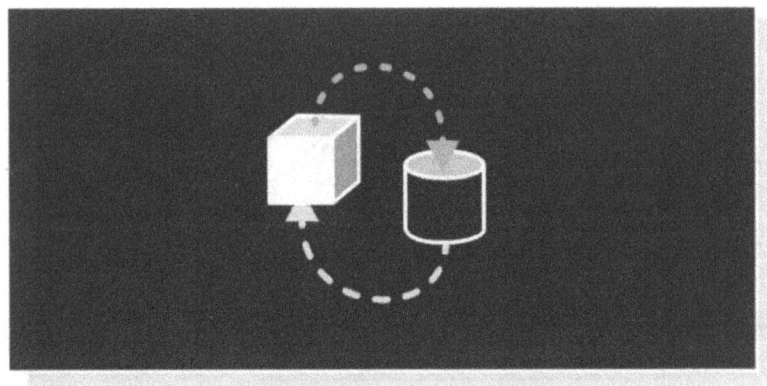

Mechanics Substitution, Changing the Existing Way of Operation

Mechanics Substitution: Substituting mechanical interactions, devices, mechanisms, and systems with fields related to objects.
Specific operations:
1. Replace mechanical systems with visual, auditory, and olfactory systems.
2. Use electric fields, magnetic fields, and electromagnetic fields to influence objects. 3. Change categories: (1) Use sports fields instead of moving fields. (2) Replace static fields with time-varying fields. (3) Replace random fields with structured fields. 4. Utilize fields and strong magnetic substances.
This is the 28th invention principle proposed by TRIZ that can solve problems.

LEO YUAN, PH.D.

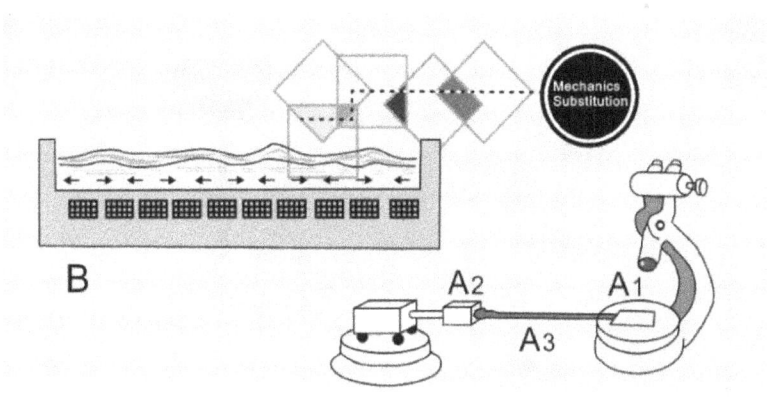

Make Good Use of Multiple Physical Effects and Integrate Them into the Existing Operating System

A: The object (A1) under the microscope can be moved with slight activation. This is achieved by the physical action of the electronic heating device (A2) and the slight expansion of the metal rod (A3).

B: A method for manufacturing polished glass plates on the surface of molten metal involves using electromagnetic waves to induce controllable corrugations on the molten metal surface. This allows the formation of corrugated glass plates on it.

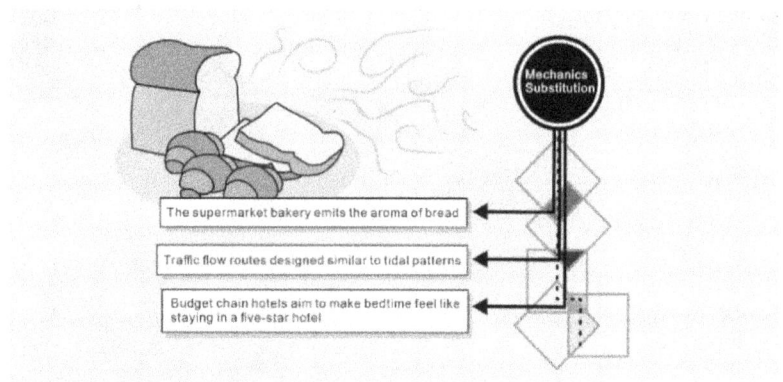

Mechanics Substitution Application Offers Various Ideas Market Applications:

1. Supermarket bakeries simulate the aroma of bread to promote sales.
2. Implementing traffic flow plans or routes similar to tidal flows to optimize peak-hour traffic.
3. Implementing a hot desk system.
4. Adopting walk-around management.
5. A CEO of a budget motel chain stated: "Our goal is that when you turn on the lights and get in bed, you feel like you're at a Hilton."

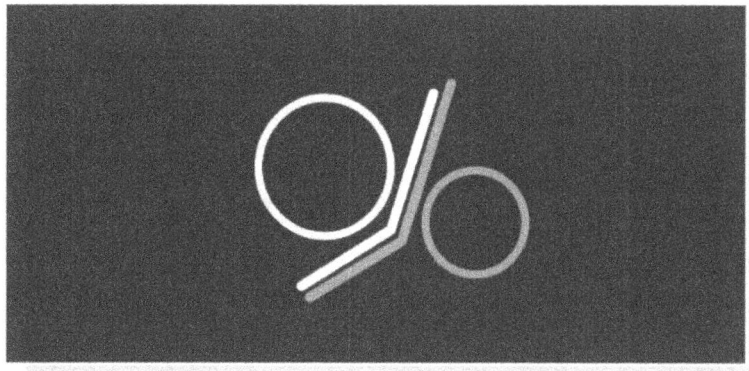

Beforehand Cushioning: Preventive Measures to Avoid Disasters

Beforehand Cushioning involves preparing in advance because nothing is perfect or entirely reliable, and precautions must be taken ahead of time.
Specific Operations: To compensate for objects with low reliability, preemptive measures can be implemented.
This is the 11th invention principle proposed by TRIZ that can solve problems.

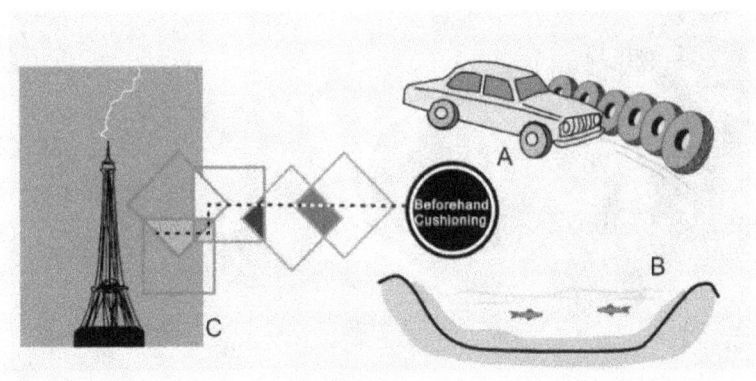

Beforehand Cushioning Can Save Many Lives!

A: In sharp turns, the car is likely to hit the mountain wall, so old tires are placed as cushions.

B: To prevent water leakage and loss in the fish pond, plastic sheeting is laid on the bottom of the pond in advance.

C: Lightning Rod: A device that receives lightning strikes, it's a metal conductor that attracts lightning current and directs it to the grounding body through the down conductor, safely discharging it into the earth.

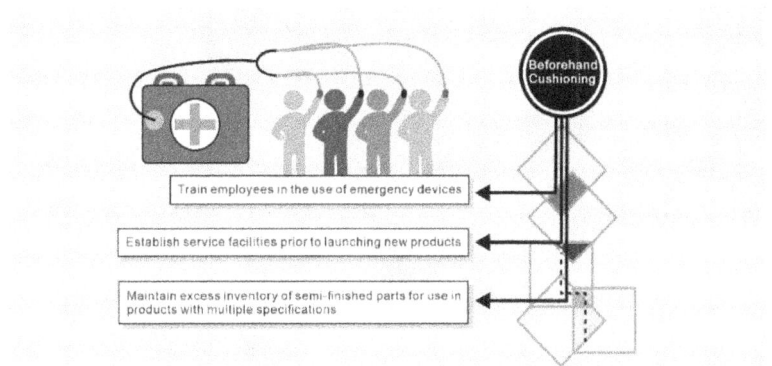

Beforehand Cushioning Application to Reduce Damage

Quality Management Applications:
1. Train employees to use emergency devices or contingency plans in case of interruptions in the commercial sales process.
2. Provide semi-finished parts or key components for use in multiple product specifications and maintain excess inventory.

Market Applications:
1. Establish service facilities before launching new products.
2. Attach a magnetized label to the product in a visible location to deter theft.

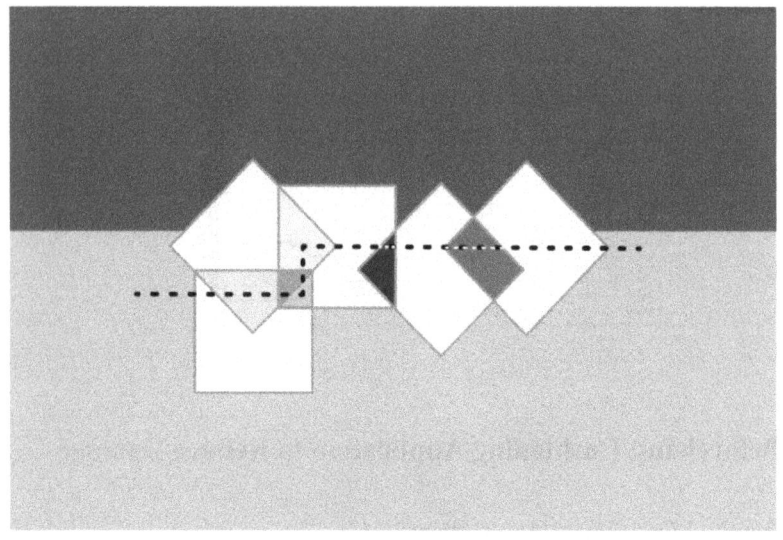

Verb Thinking Cross-Border Association

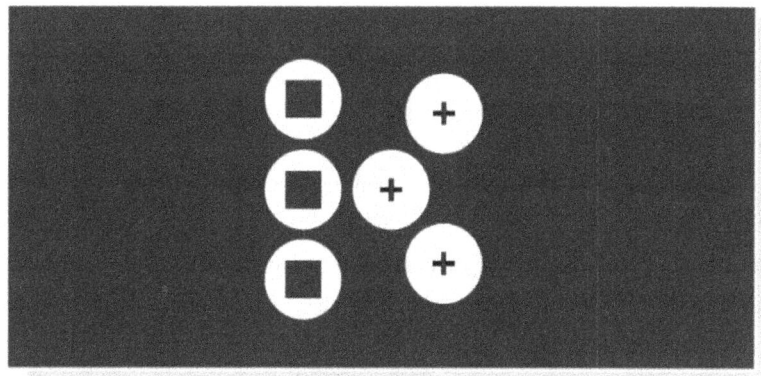

Put to Other Uses?

What new, more appropriate use could there be? What would be its improved use?

This is the first self-question posed by Alex F. Osborn to trigger creativity, echoing Tago Akira's fourth thinking rule of "association" and "CON" Connect for generating new ideas.

Can Waste Paper Be Used for Other Purposes?

Waste paper doesn't just have to be thrown away; recycling is also an option. What other uses could it have?

1. There is a waste paper charcoal-making machine. The waste paper is soaked in water for 24 hours, removed, and placed into the machine. The water is squeezed out, the paper is pressed into cubes, and then dried in the shade to produce highly flammable paper charcoal. Each piece can burn for up to one and a half hours.

2. Steam the waste paper, cut it into long strips, knead it into small paper balls, add nutrients, and use it as feed for cattle and sheep. Animals fed with this nutritious paper-based feed gain significant weight due to improved digestion and absorption.

3. Waste paper can be recycled into notebooks, paper flowers, sheet or granular cushioning materials, absorbents, and even furniture.

Does this make sense? By playing this association game with any random item, you can enhance your creativity. Over time, your ability to make connections will improve significantly, allowing you to think more comprehensively about things in the future.

LEO YUAN, PH.D.

Can newspapers be used for other purposes?

Based on the "Unusual Uses of Newspapers" experiment published by Xu Zhijun, Chen Xuezhi, and Qiu Fazhong (2012) in the "Journal of Creation," this paper compiled the originality scores for various uses of newspapers. Participants were given scores based on how easy or difficult it was to associate a particular use with newspapers: very easy (0 points), somewhat difficult (1 point), and very difficult (2 points). Below is a table summarizing these scores. You can either conduct your own test or simply browse to appreciate the less obvious uses of newspapers.

Originality and association are crucial concepts. In "The Medici Effect," it is noted that chef Marcus Samuelsson possesses a low association barrier, enabling him to form unconventional connections beyond the realm of Swedish cuisine. Conversely, many individuals have high association barriers, often limiting them to conventional ideas.

When Marcus Samuelsson contemplates tomatoes, his thoughts extend far beyond the scope of most Swedish or European chefs. For instance, when author Frans Johansson mentioned pesto, Marcus Samuelsson didn't think of basil but rather suggested fennel. Similarly, if the topic is a tandoor oven, Marcus Samuelsson immediately associates it not with chicken but with smoked salmon.

This demonstrates that individuals with strong association skills are more likely to conceive surprising ideas, as they can easily think of things that ordinary people have not considered. Naturally, what they create may not initially be recognized by others, which exemplifies creativity.

This underscores the importance of nurturing originality and association skills. Let's begin with the use of "newspaper" now! I'll give you 5 minutes to write down as many uses as you can and tally your points. Keep this test paper and take another test in six months. This simple exercise helps evaluate your originality and association skills over time.

Advancing the Medici Fusion

Category	Use	Fraction
Music	Make sound effects, as a musical instrument	2
	Fold into baton, trumpet	2
	Makes a scary explosion	2

Category	Use	Fraction
Stationery	Practice calligraphy, POP word	0
	Calculation paper, note, note paper	0
	Doily (write calligraphy, paint watercolor, write poster)	0
	Cutting mat; cut words, write letters, write articles	1
	As a book cover	1
	Black pigment, pencil, pen tube	2
	Mouse pad, backing plate, cut font	2
	Construction paper, wall newspaper	2
	Envelope, pen holder, bookmark, watercolor pen	2

Category	Use	Fraction
Have fun	Airplane, ball, group games	0
	Children's play, stationery, boat	1
	Word games such as word guessing and word finding	1
	Do magic, bat, kite	1
	Cheer stick, colored balls	2
	Knife, sword, gun	2

	A prank made into a hood to scare people	2
	Hula hoop, mahjong cloth	2
	Place it far away as a shooting target	2
	Paper lantern, massage stick	2
	Puzzle, gag	2
	Make a circle and throw it at others	2
	Create smoke, muscle training	2
	Blowpipe, model, mummy	2
	Cut holes to make decoding boards	2
	Baton, sky lampshade	2

Category	Use	Fraction
Study	Clippings	0
	Literacy, recognize words, check, gather information, picture	1
	Hand in homework, write literature	1
	Read aloud, reading ability training, writing ability	2
	Teaching materials, contribute, geometric figures drill	2
	Read newspapers to learn typesetting, learn foreign languages by reading foreign language newspapers	2
	Take a copy and take a photo to prove the date	2
	Cheat sheet, high school basic test guessing questions	2

Advancing the Medici Fusion

Category	Use	Fraction
Science	Loudspeaker, telescope	2
	Microphone, do experiments	2
	Measure the size of the floor, ruler	2

Category	Use	Fraction
Art and decoration	Package, wrapping paper, origami, art and crafts, art materials	0
	Decoration, props, prop filler	0
	Collage, peel-and-stick art, card, draw, graffiti	1
	Work or work aids, lay out the venue	1
	Installation art	1
	Paper cutting, handicrafts, artwork, artistic creation	2
	Paper art, mask, poster, embossed, pressed plant specimens	2
	Floral, viscose, rubbing, origami flower, woven material	2
	Ribbon, tassel, cut and paste, origami crane, fold stars	2
	When firing pottery, place it in a container to prevent deformation, bag pattern	2
	Sticky board, glue multiple layers of paint to make utensils	2
	Gift box, mural	2

Category	Use	Fraction

Category	Use	Fraction
Cooking	Table runner, napkin, placemat	0
	Insulation pads, cover instant noodles, vegetable	0
	Picnic towel, BBQ seat cushion	1
	Filter paper, apron, funnel	2
	Picnic, for barbecue, paper pot	2
	Cup, straw, cork	2
	Toothpick, knife sharpening	2

Category	Use	Fraction
Furniture And daily necessities	Chair cushion, cushion	0
	Fan, table legs	0
	Wallpaper, pave wall, shoe stretch	0
	Carton, basket, carpet	1
	Table, chair, foot pad	1
	Curtain, door curtain	1
	Mattress, straw mat, pillow	2
	Partition, elevate, insole	2
	Spread on the ground to place things	2
	Cabinet mat, rope, coat hanger	2
	Window, mosquito coil pad	2
	Paper door, cabinet, crutch	2
	Put something in the box	2
	Made into long cardboard without asking for help	2
	Accumulate into piles and act as heavy objects	2
	Made into transport belt	2

Category	Use	Fraction
Reproduce	Recycle and sell for money, recycle, recycled paper	0
	Pulp	1
	Extract edible substances for meals	2
	Items made from waste	2

Category	Use	Fraction
Feed	Pet (bird, dog, cat, mouse) litter	1
	Pet (dog, cat) to the restroom, as a potted plant, Hit pets	2
	Fertilizer, sheep food, Training a dog to pick up newspapers	2
	Use tape to tie newspapers into small balls to play with cats and dogs	2

Category	Use	Fraction
Wear	Clothing, hat, crown	0
	Shoe, slippers, Grass skirts, wig, cloak, Gloves	2
	Bag, eye mask, necklace, glasses frames, hood	2
	Wristband, Headband	2

Category	Use	Fraction
Arms	Fight insects, cockroach, fly, mosquito	0
	Beat someone, stick, Threatening	0

	letter	
	Beat little kid, arson, Roll up and shoot someone, kidnap someone	2
	Throw the police	2

Category	Use	Fraction
Cover	Sunshade, block light, block the wind	0
	Keep out the rain, umbrella, raincoat	0
	Glass (maintain privacy)	1
	Repair window holes	1
	Block body, Keep away insects	2
	Disinfect covered items	2
	Camouflage	2

Category	Use	Fraction
Protect	Packed lunch, fruit, fish	0
	Filler, buffer	0
	Fragile items (glass, light bulbs, porcelain, wine bottles...)	0
	Cover broken glass, porcelain, tableware, dustproof	0
	Packing things, belongings, moisture-proof	1
	Anti-skid, shockproof, anti-collision, book wrapping, dangerous goods wrapping	2
	Pack valuables to prevent injuries, Cash included (to protect against bad guys)	2

Advancing the Medici Fusion

	Get the ladder to get the bed in the dormitory, pest control	2

Category	Use	Fraction
Insulation	Quilt for warmth	0
	Pack frozen food, rice balls, lunch boxes, and keep fresh	0
	Keep pets out of the cold, wrap fruits and vegetables to make them ripe faster	2
	Make a fire to keep warm	2

Category	Use	Fraction
Combustion	Make a fire, help burn	0
	Make fire by fan, fire lead	2

Category	Use	Fraction
Mood	Tear up paper to vent your emotions	1
	Send secret messages	2

Category	Use	Fraction
Wipe	Toilet paper, glass cleaning	0
	Diaper	0
	Rag	1
	Mop, clean	2
	Clean the table, clean glasses	2
	Cleaning windows, scraping shoes and poop	2

	Shine your shoes, put up a screen on the window, and use a vacuum cleaner on the other side to suck up the dust	2
	Wipe dirt on desktop screen	2

Category	Use	Fraction
Clean	Pack garbage, kitchen waste, trash cans, garbage boxes	0
	Garbage bags, lining trash cans, and eating steak to block the squirting juice	0
	Pack pet waste	0
	Cut or dye your hair to pad your shoulders	1
	Cut nails and put them underneath, paint the floor	2
	Paint cap, fold into a thin stick to clean the grooves, tear into small strips and turn into a whisk, put under the carpet of the car	2
	Make garbage	2

Category	Use	Fraction
Adsorption	Water absorption, desiccant, dehumidification	0
	Deodorize	0
	Smoke, smoke oil	1
	Mouth water when playing a musical	2

	instrument, water from shoes on rainy days	
	Newspapers can be used to absorb what is commonly known as oil film on the water surface of the fish tank	2

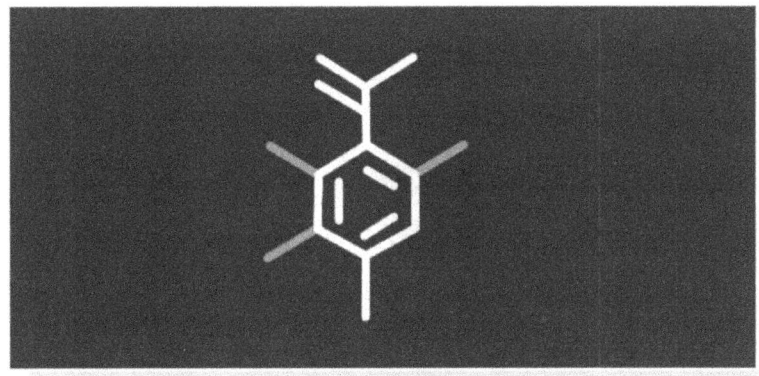

Adapt?

Is there anything similar? What other ideas does this provide? Has anything like this been done before? What can I learn from those who came before me? How can I surpass them?

This is Alex F. Osborn's second self-question that can spark creativity.

Advancing the Medici Fusion

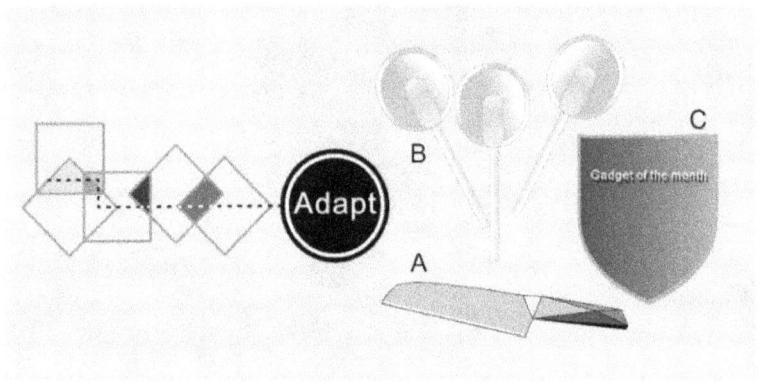

By Modifying an Object, You Can Enhance Its Functionality

A: A kitchen knife that doesn't need sharpening for 25 years. Titanium carbide is melted at the speed of laser light at over 4000 degrees Celsius, and the blade is coated with a special coating.

B: Lollipops that are delicious and tooth-friendly. Transform sugar-free lollipops into dental care treats.

C: This month's popular book can inspire this month's ideas and transform them into this month's fruits, candies, collectibles, and the "Gadget of the Month" club.

Modify?

New changes? Adjust plans, colors, movements, sounds, smells, shapes? Any other changes?
This is Alex F. Osborn's third self-question that can spark creativity.

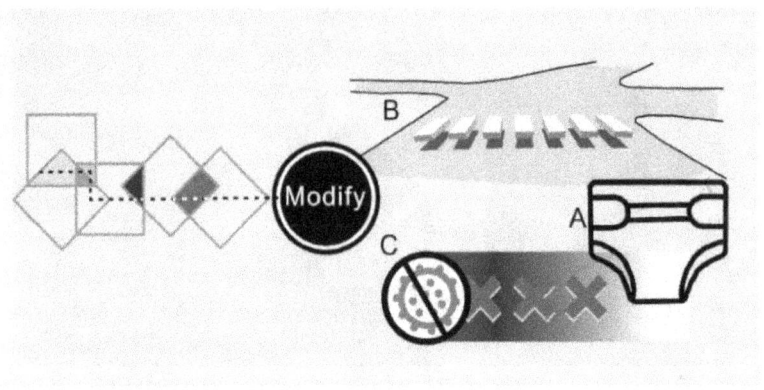

Modify Existing Items Slightly to Create New Ideas or Functions

A: Transform diapers into diaper underwear, which resemble regular underwear for toilet training, encouraging babies to practice without wearing diapers.

B: Implement zebra crossings with three-dimensional driftwood visual effects to attract drivers' attention and reduce their speed.

C: In the brewing industry, Pasteur discovered that certain temperatures can kill microorganisms without affecting the aroma of wine. This method is also applicable to milk sterilization, potentially saving many lives.

LEO YUAN, PH.D.

Magnify?

What can be added? More time? Increased frequency? Greater strength? Higher intensity? Longer duration? Thicker volume? Enhanced value? Addition of new ingredients? Cloning? Multiplication? Exaggeration?
This is the fourth self-question posed by Alex F. Osborn to stimulate creativity. It also echoes Tago Akira's "PUP" (Pile Up) principle for generating new ideas.

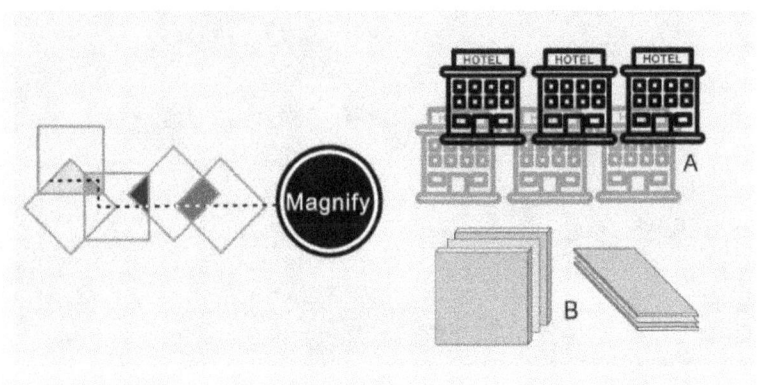

Buy One, Get One Free, or Even Double the Offer, as Long as There Is Profit to Be Made

A: Buy one night and get one night free at a European hotel, stay three nights and get three free at a Japanese chain hotel.

B: Applying a layer of adhesive material between glass layers creates laminated glass, known as safety glass, which enhances impact resistance.

LEO YUAN, PH.D.

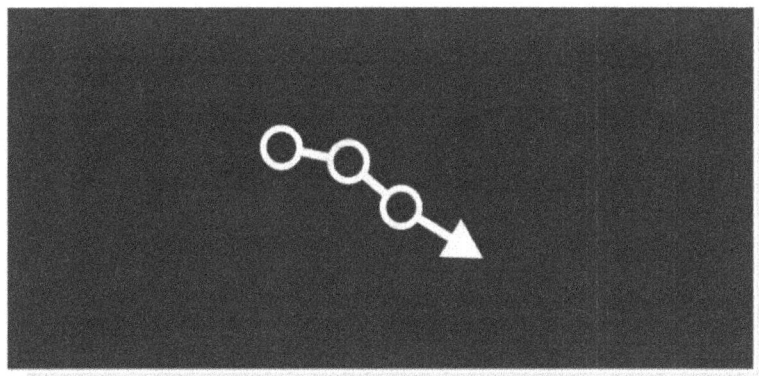

Minify?

What can be reduced? Less? Compressed? Shrink? Lowered? Shorter? Lighter? Deleted? Streamlined? Segmented? Implicit?

This is the fifth self-question posed by Alex F. Osborn to spark creativity, and it also aligns with the seventh thinking rule "OMIT" proposed by Tago Akira for generating new ideas.

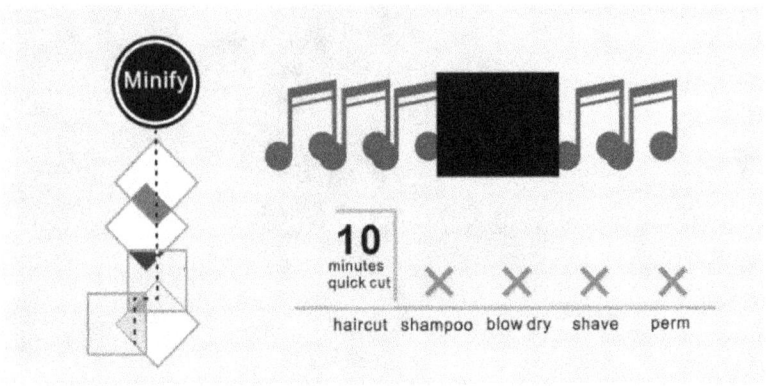

It May Be Better to Reduce Unnecessary Elements and Aim for Conciseness and Clarity

1. Quiet shopping hour: Switch to a low-sensory mode by dimming the lights and turning off the music. This provides a conducive environment for autistic children and consumers who prefer silence in supermarkets.
2. Quick-cut barber shop: Offers a 10-minute service focusing solely on hair cutting, omitting washing, blow-drying, shaving, and perming. This approach emphasizes speed and affordability.

Substitute?

Who or what can replace it? What alternative ingredients, methods, forces, places, or possibilities are there? Any other explanations?

This is the sixth self-question proposed by Alex F. Osborn to stimulate creativity. It also aligns with the 11th thinking rule "IC" (Interchange) proposed by Tago Akira for generating new ideas.

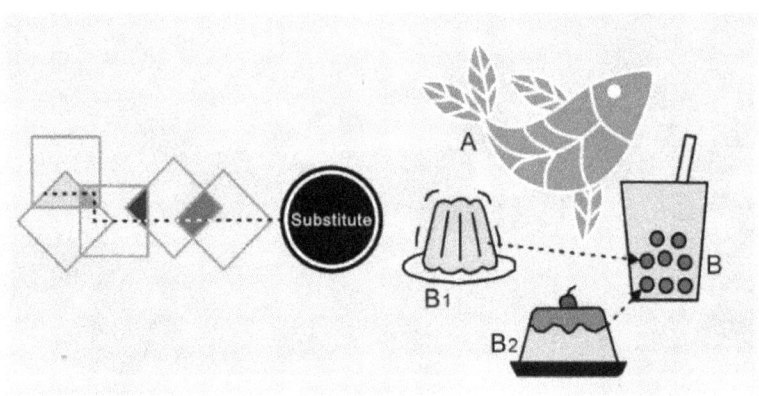

Substitute Different Ingredients to Taste Fresher and Possibly Healthier

A: Plant-based meat substitutes processed artificial meat. In vegetarian restaurants, the dishes closely resemble those in regular restaurants, featuring faux caviar, steak, and salmon roe, all prepared in vegetarian versions.

B: Use different ingredients to replace pearl milk tea; for example, substitute B1 jelly or B2 pudding for tapioca pearls, and use coconut milk or soy milk instead of dairy milk.

Rearrange?

Swapping ingredients? Different forms? Alternative configurations? Rearranging order? Changing causation? Adjusting steps? Modifying schedule?

This is Alex F. Osborn's seventh self-question that can spark creativity.

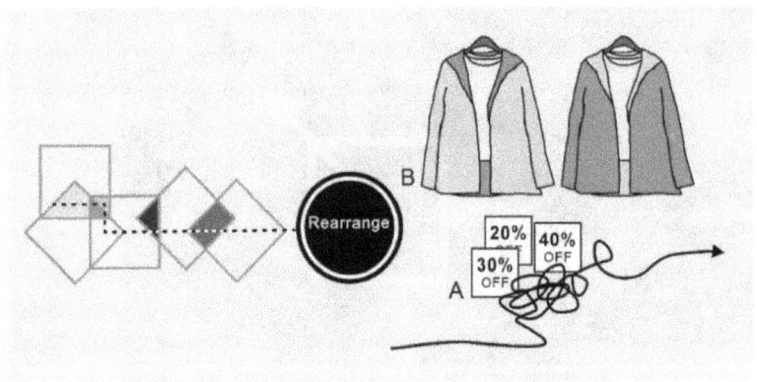

As Soon as You Encounter Any Inconvenience, Rearrange It!

A: In stores, place ultra-low-priced discounted products in piles where customer traffic is highest. This helps slow down the flow, giving consumers more time to view the original products in the area.

B: A reversible jacket can be worn either side out, offering two different looks.

Reverse?

Change the original status from affirmation to negation, or consider the opposite? Turn things around? Switch sides? Reverse the top and bottom? Swap roles? Compare one's feelings with another's? Change seats?

These are the eighth self-questioning techniques proposed by Alex F. Osborn that can trigger creativity. They also align with the ninth thinking rule "REV" (Reverse) proposed by Tago Akira for generating new ideas.

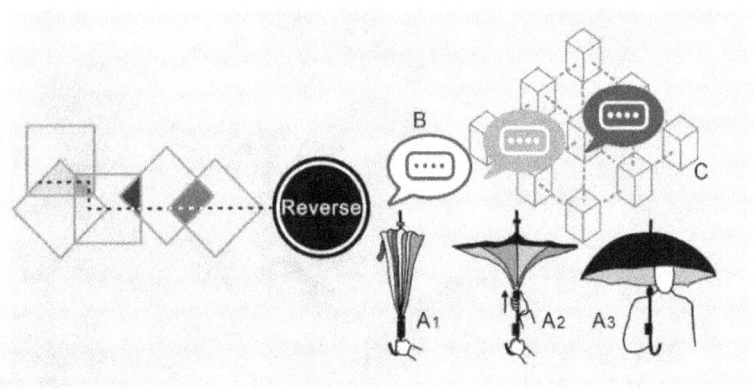

The Umbrella Opens in a Reverse Direction, Saving Effort and Providing Convenience

A: The structure of the reverse-opening umbrella is similar to that of a traditional umbrella. It is inverted (A1), pushed up (A2), and held open (A3). B: Social software automatically deletes message tracks after a certain time. By reversing this idea, call records are stored on the blockchain (C) and cannot be deleted, which could be applicable to legal documents.

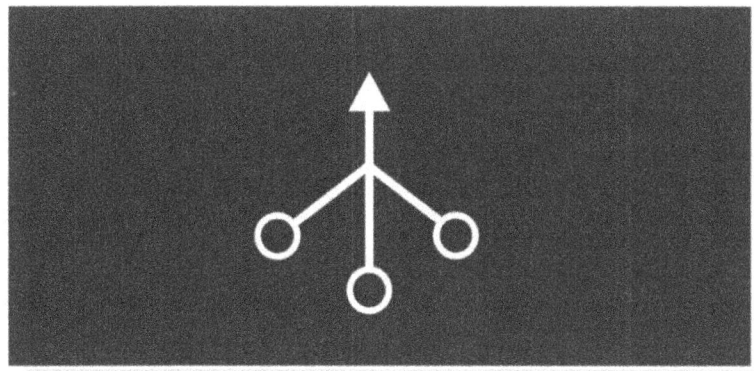

Combine?

Mix? Combination? Classification? Complete set? Combined unit? Effectiveness of combination? Requirements for combinations? Combinatorial thinking?

These are nine self-questioning techniques proposed by Alex F. Osborn that can trigger creativity. They also correspond to the fifth thinking rule "COM" (Combine) proposed by Tago Akira for generating new ideas.

Advancing the Medici Fusion

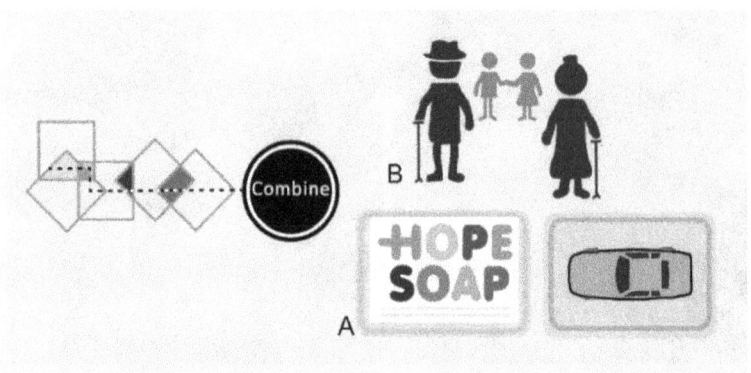

The Old Man Tells Stories to the Young Children, and Both Groups Benefit from Each Other

A: With Hope Soap, toys can be retrieved after the soap is used.
B: In a nursing home's kindergarten, elderly residents tell stories to children every day.

Add?

Add functions that have never been thought of before, or add new objects to any material.

Innovative additions: Add a pencil holder to the pencil and incorporate a filter into the cigarette.

Transplantation and addition: Attach folding benches and small hooks to the ladder.

Main body additions: Integrate a timer, water temperature gauge, lint suction disk, anti-twist device, and a small-item washing net bag into the washing machine.

This is Tago Akira's second thinking rule, "ADD," which he proposes for developing new brewing concepts.

Advancing the Medici Fusion

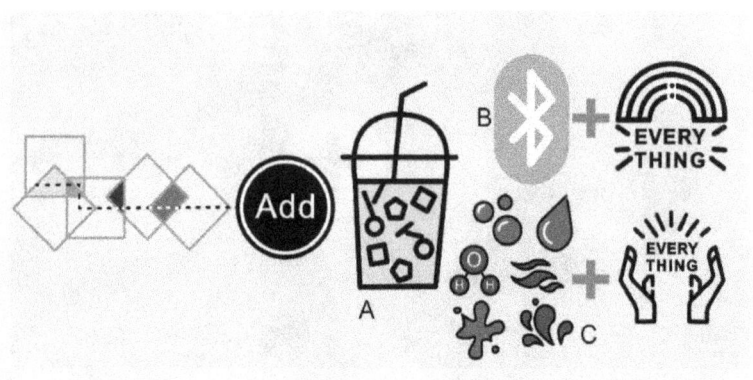

New Functions Can Be Added to a Wide Range of Product Usage Scenarios

A: A drink designed to improve allergies is a light Kampo product available at convenience stores.

B: Integrate Bluetooth with various products. Any product should consider adding Bluetooth functionality to extend its original purpose.

C: Explore "Liquid + [a]" modes, such as turning object [a] into a liquid or combining object [a] with other liquids. Examples include liquid + pork floss, barbecue sauce + [a], salad dressing + [a], liquid + vitamins, etc.

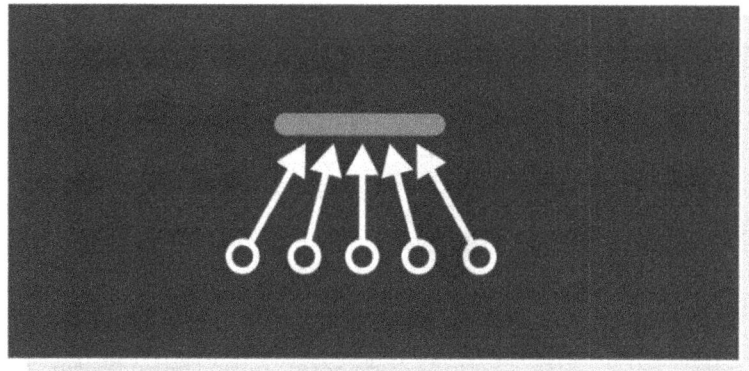

Organize?

Summarizing each element together, or classifying and grouping each element, and looking at the general trend or direction from an overall perspective will generate a different view and possibly foster creativity.

This is the third thinking rule "ORG" Organize, proposed by Tago Akira for developing new concepts.

By Summarizing and Analyzing Various Types of Food, You Can Create an Automatic Cooking Mode

A: A theme park that allows children to experience various professions. It can realistically recreate 50 workplaces, each about two-thirds the actual size. They can role-play as firefighters or police officers.

B: An automatic humidity sensing control device. After studying the ingredients of each dish, controlling the combination of materials, and conducting experiments to find the best cooking mode, the best-selling electronic pot was launched at that time.

Divide?

What appears to be two interrelated things may actually be separate independent entities. An integrated unit can also be broken down into several smaller units, and the cumulative functions of each small unit may exceed those of the integrated unit.

Separation can also be considered as partitioning or decomposing into numerous smaller units, or detaching from a specific unit. This change in the whole can lead to an entirely new situation.

This is Tago Akira's sixth thinking rule "DIV" (Divide), which proposes a new brewing concept.

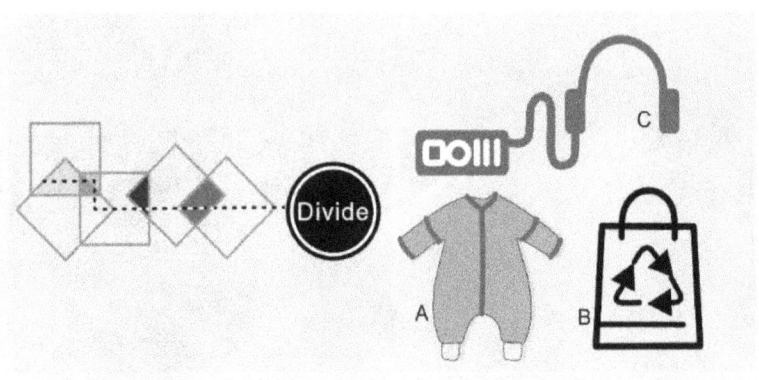

If You Consider a Walkman That Only Plays Music, You'll Appreciate the Benefits of Specialization

A: A sleeping bag with a split-leg design tightly wraps both legs to keep them warm.

B: Bags made from various agricultural products that can be eaten or decompose on their own are environmentally friendly.

C: The Walkman is a device used exclusively for listening to music. Similarly, other single-function devices include recorders, translators, and scanners.

Focus?

Thinking about where the focus of something lies, or identifying key processes, involves pinpointing a small, critical area to seek breakthroughs. In other words, narrowing down the focus to the correct target is the essence of focusing.

Focused thinking is goal-oriented thinking. When goals are set accurately, creativity naturally emerges. For example, a restaurant's goal might be to cater to small families post-war, where a couple and two children can easily dine together weekly. This clear goal guides subsequent decisions on pricing, menu offerings, and environment planning.

This is the 8th thinking rule "FOCUS" proposed by Tago Akira for developing new brewing ideas.

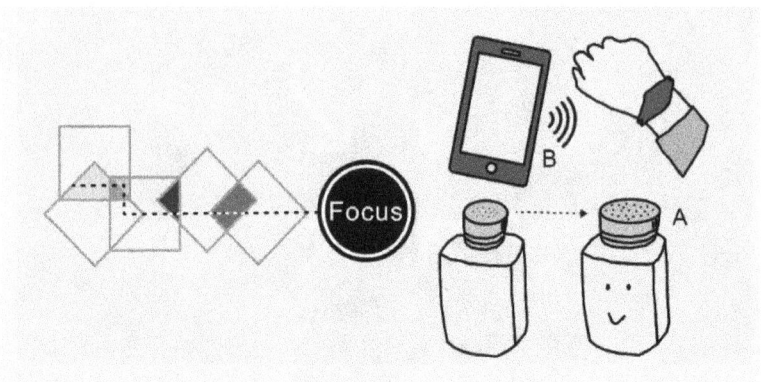

By Focusing on the Marketing Result You Want to Achieve, You Can Capture the Key Points

A: To enhance performance, a MSG company's solution was to enlarge the hole in the inner cap of the MSG bottle and increase the number of holes. This change naturally increased consumers' usage of MSG.

B: Use Bluetooth to connect the mobile phone with the anti-lost bracelet for children.

LEO YUAN, PH.D.

Slide?

When faced with a problem, looking at it from a different perspective often provides unexpected insights. For instance, viewing the street from a child's height may reveal issues where adults have designed public facilities without considering children's actual needs. Examples include public telephones with coin slots positioned too high, elevator buttons on upper floors of tall buildings placed out of reach, and even doorbells positioned too high at home. This is the 10th thinking rule "SLIDE" proposed by Tago Akira for generating new brewing ideas.

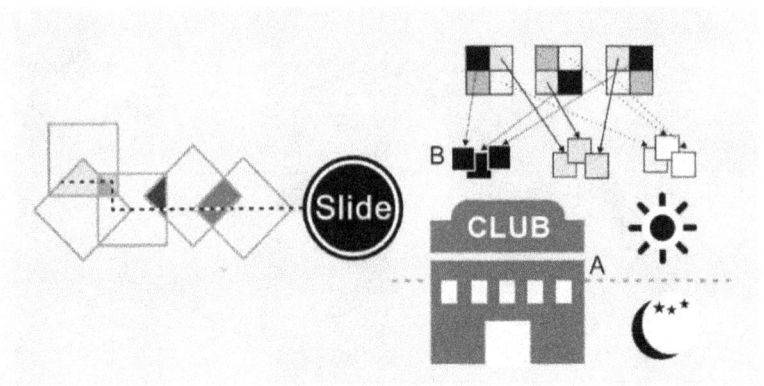

Time Sharing or Batch Traveling Are All Extensions of Slide

A: Time sharing allows access to clubs, yachts, and gyms at different times. B: Each department is required to send one employee weekly on cross-department camping trips. Over the course of a year, this fosters better interdepartmental relationships and enhances both horizontal and vertical communication.

LEO YUAN, PH.D.

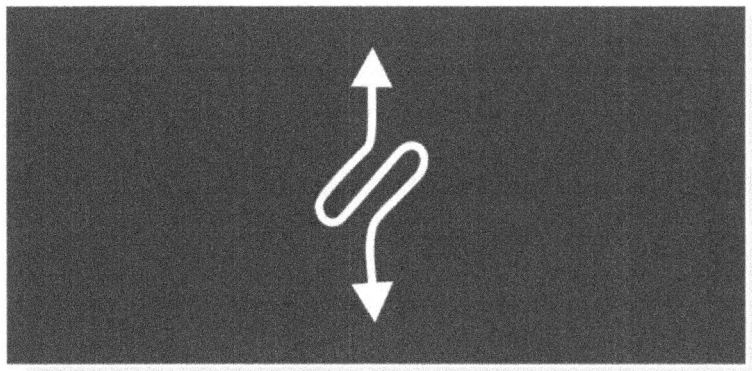

Expand?

Expand a specific factor, activate your observational powers, and utilize the thinking principles you've mastered to their fullest potential.

This is Tago Akira's 12th thinking rule "EXP" for proposing new brewing concepts.

Advancing the Medici Fusion

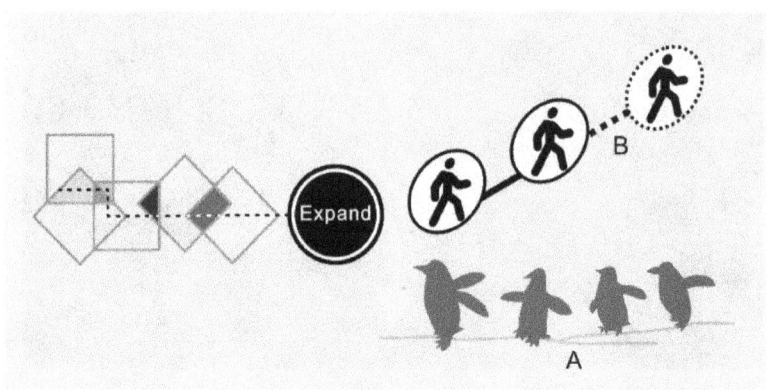

The Penguin Parade is a Classic Example of Expand

A: The zoo's Penguin Parade has evolved from a static display to an interactive experience. The penguins now move actively, parading regularly each day, allowing visitors to observe them up close.

B: Using a disabled card sensor extends the green light duration for pedestrians.

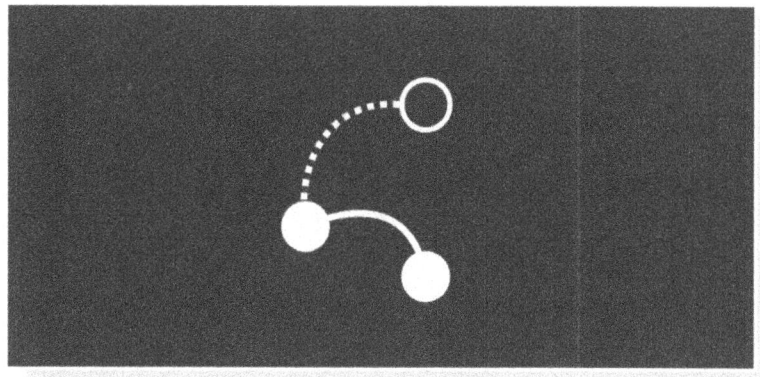

Detour? If You Take a Longer Detour First and Then Return, You May Gain More

Sometimes, the longer route can be shorter than the shortcut. For example, leather produced domestically is first exported for sale abroad and then imported back. This often results in it being preferred by domestic consumers due to its popularity abroad.

This is Tago Akira's 13th thinking rule "DET" Detour, proposed for a new brewing concept.

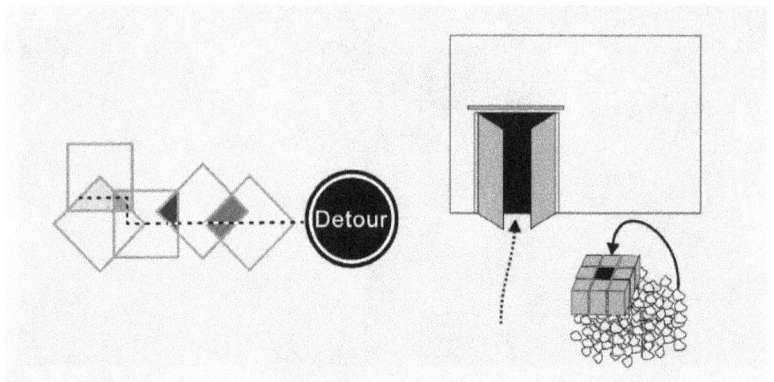

The Restaurant Deliberately Doesn't Let You Open the Door and Enter Directly, But Instead It Has Become Popular!

The restaurant's door cannot be opened directly. There is a secret method near the door to open it. You might throw a stone into a cave or place your hand in the mouth of a stone animal, and the door will open.

This indirect way of entering does not require advertising because people will spread the word. They will tell their friends, showcasing that they are in the know about cool and new things.

Other examples include holding a historical food and cuisine exhibition to explore history through the ingredients people consumed at that time.

Play?

Gamification marketing involves capturing the interesting elements and mechanics of games, integrating them into your business field, and applying them. Commonly used elements include rankings, medals, points, levels, tasks, random rewards, etc.

An easy-going gaming mentality can often spark fresh ideas.

This is Tago Akira's 14th thinking rule, "PLAY", when he proposes a new brewing concept.

Turn Promotions into Games and Incorporate Bonuses. This Makes It Much More Interesting

A: Lucky Roulette: Accumulate a certain amount of points to get a chance to win in the roulette lottery. Or, when purchasing specific goods or drinks in the store, you can spin the lucky wheel to receive different discounts or even items for free.

B: Red Envelope Rain: Red envelopes will be distributed on the webpage at noon.

Return to Basics?

When your thinking reaches a dead end, return to the starting point and begin anew.
1. Rediscover the original meaning or explore new aspects from existing facts. For example, a detective revisits the crime scene after handling the case.
2. When you've pondered deeply and find yourself stuck in a mental maze, clear your mind of previous thoughts and start fresh. Return to the root of the problem. For instance, when planning an advertising project, revisit the market site to gain clarity.
This is the 15th rule of 'RTB' thinking in Tago Akira's new concept of brewing: Return to Basics.

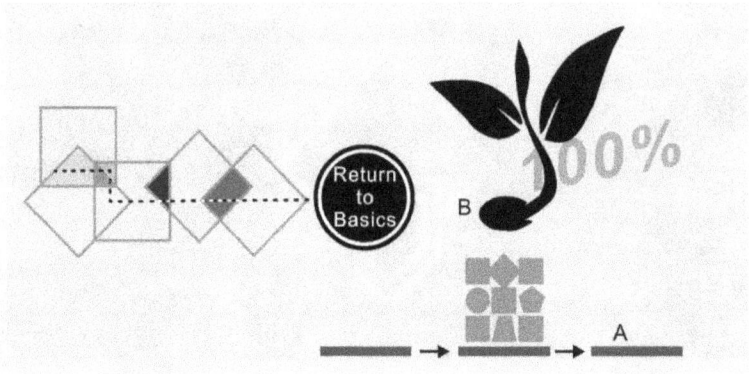

If You Carefully Consider the Design of "Restoring the Entire Original State," New Ideas Will Emerge

A: A detachable sports venue can be dismantled after the game and used for other construction purposes. The land can then be restored to its original appearance. Designing a modular set that can be moved and assembled locally for each sports event or relocated to another location or country can significantly reduce construction costs.

B: Vegetables grown in greenhouses require no washing at all. They are grown without the use of pesticides throughout the entire process, ensuring they are healthy, non-toxic, and ready to enjoy directly at the table.

LEO YUAN, PH.D.

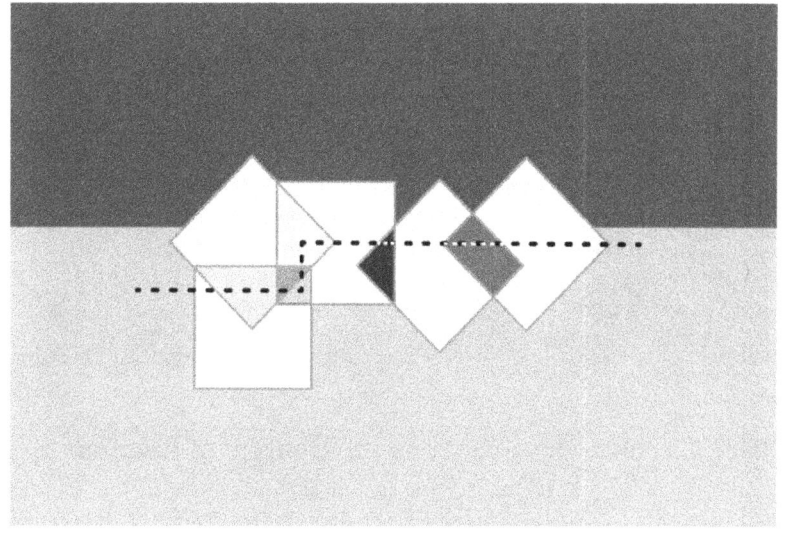

Set Theme Cross-Border Association

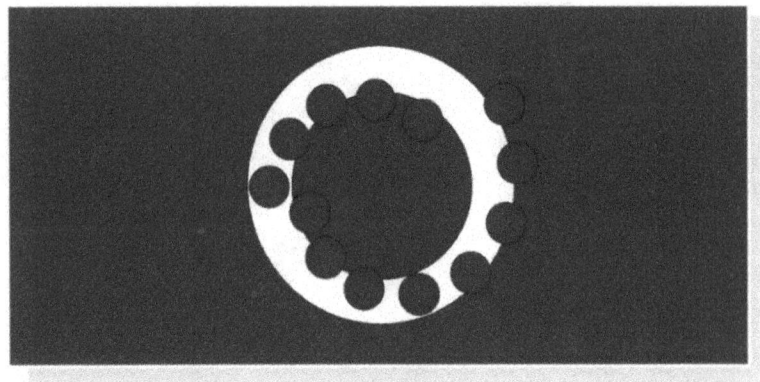

Disc? Circular Movement and the Concept of Rotation

Taking the theme of "circular motion" as an example, many natural phenomena exhibit circular shapes and movements, such as the orbits of the sun and moon, the shape of eggs, tornadoes, and more. Human beings have long been fascinated by circular motion. By exploring this theme, one might consider the practicality of transforming various processes into circular operations.

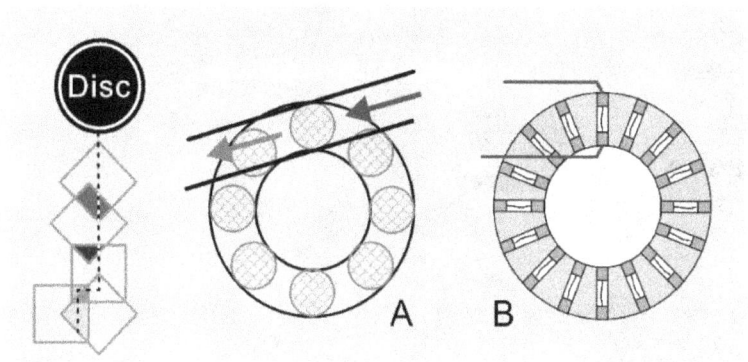

Equipment for Rotating Discs to Maintain Uninterrupted Operations

A: In disc-type filters, when the filter becomes clogged with impurities, it can be immediately replaced with a new one by rotating it. This design ensures continuous filtration without interrupting production.

B: In disc-type fuses, once a fuse burns out, simply rotate it and replace it with a new one to restore functionality.

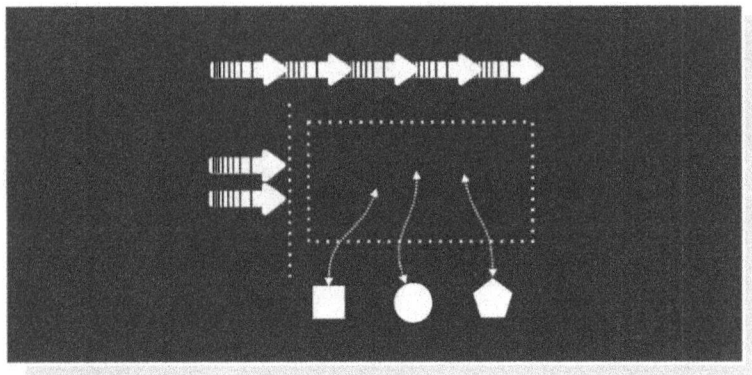

Heat Conduction: Utilizing it to Accelerate or Create Obstacles

Some entities can move swiftly yet encounter impediments at certain junctures. We must delve into the reasons for these halts and explore them through the lens of physical chemistry. Most transformations in entities are intricately tied to principles of physical chemistry. Identifying the key factors causing these halts may potentially lead to innovative developments.

LEO YUAN, PH.D.

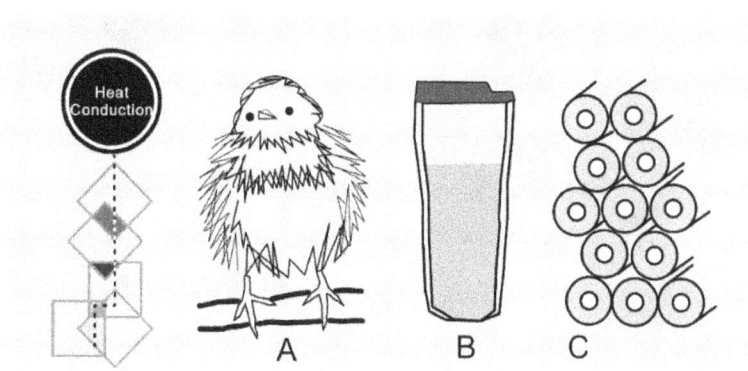

Thermal Conductivity: Applications in Robins, Thermos Bottles, and Thermal Gauze

The thermal conductivity coefficient varies widely across different materials: diamond registers up to 2300 W/m·K, copper 401 W/m·K, and air a mere 0.026 W/m·K, indicating poor heat conduction through air. This characteristic can be effectively utilized in various applications.

A: During winter, a robin's feathers are fluffy and warm, with air trapped between them. This layer of air, which has poor heat conductivity, prevents the escape of body heat.

B: A thermos bottle typically consists of two layers of plastic with an air gap in between. This design ensures that hot coffee remains hot for longer as the heat struggles to conduct through the air gap.

C: Hollow fiber textiles use air trapped within their structure to impede the transfer of heat energy.

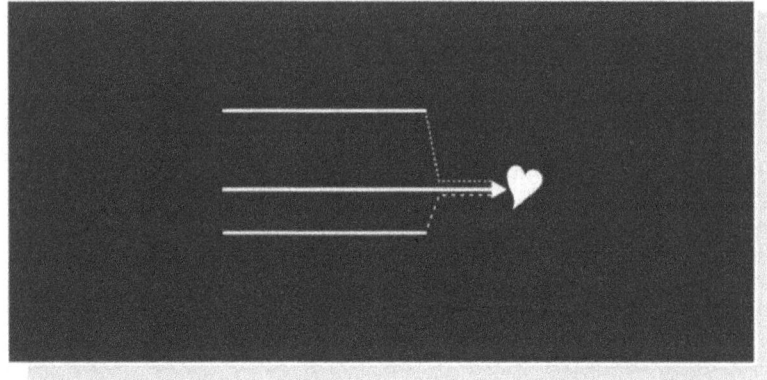

No Matter What You Do, The Most Fundamental Aspect is to Consider the Actual Needs

Carefully identifying the genuine needs of consumers is crucial. Aligning your offerings precisely with what consumer desire is key to sparking their buying and usage motivation. Therefore, regardless of your strategy, you must engage with the market, interact with consumers, and uncover their latent needs. Often, consumers may not articulate their needs clearly, so the first to discern these needs will likely emerge as the initial winner.

LEO YUAN, PH.D.

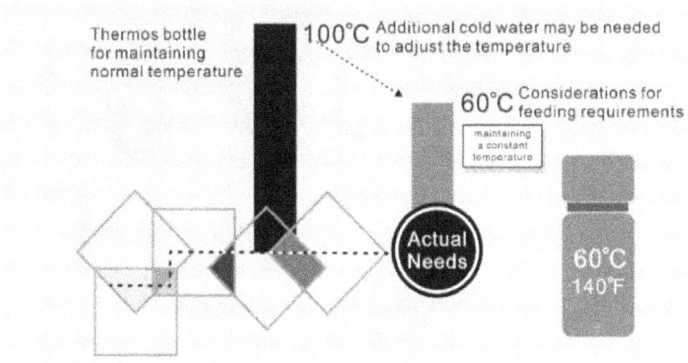

Understanding Mothers' Actual Demand for Preparing Milk Allows Manufacturers to Profit Significantly

When designing thermoses, the usual approach is to heat water to 100 degrees Celsius and then cool it to 90 degrees Celsius. While this suits most people, it's unsuitable for mothers caring for babies, as it washes away the nutrients in baby formula. After cooling to 60 degrees Celsius, the water becomes suitable for baby consumption.

Recognizing that mothers require water at precisely 60 degrees Celsius for mixing formula, thermos bottles are now being designed to maintain a constant temperature of 60 degrees Celsius. This allows mothers to pour out water and immediately prepare baby formula without further temperature adjustment.

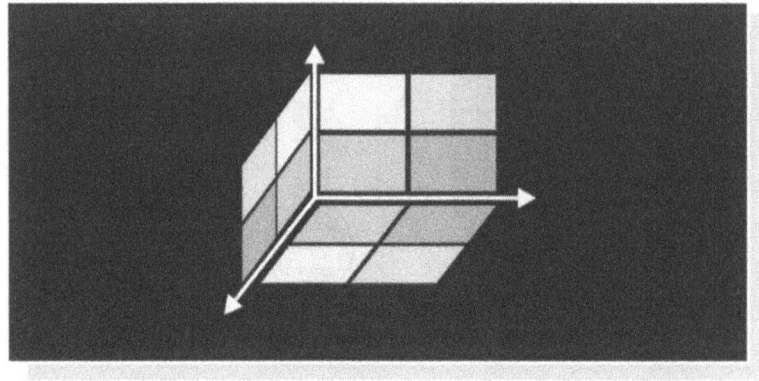

Matrix Thinking Enables the Analysis and Organization of Situations, Thereby Enhancing Work Efficiency

By considering the X and Y axes, situations can be categorized into four quadrants based on these two aspects alone. Adding a Z axis introduces another dimension, creating additional quadrants. Certain complex situations benefit from this three-dimensional matrix approach.

LEO YUAN, PH.D.

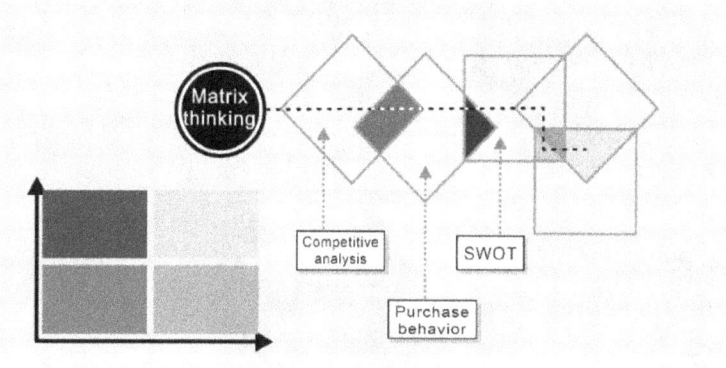

There Are Three Common Methods of Matrix Thinking

1. SWOT Analysis: Strengths, Weaknesses, Opportunities, and Threats are used to conduct an in-depth and comprehensive analysis of oneself and competitive positioning before formulating a development strategy.
2. BCG Matrix: Dogs, Cash Cows, Stars, and Question Marks serve as guidance and a basis for judgment within the enterprise for evaluating the existing product portfolio and allocating resources to business units.
3. FCB Grid: This categorizes consumer purchasing decision-making models based on the buyer's "High Involvement - Low Involvement" (X-axis) and "Think - Feel" (Y-axis). It initially classifies four types: fully informed, emotional purchasing, habitual buying, and impulsive buying.

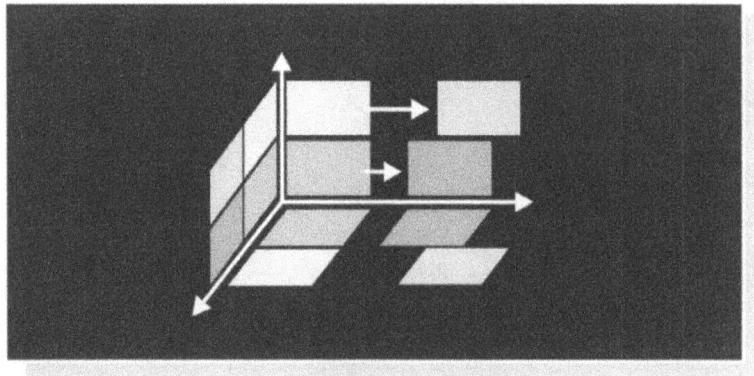

Matrix Evolution, Combined with the Element of Time, Becomes a Dynamic Structural Analysis

When dynamic or time factors are incorporated, this matrix serves another purpose: it can anticipate future conflicts or overlaps between situations. Additionally, it allows for the dynamic rehearsal of all elements in three-dimensional space to fully grasp the situation and achieve the goal of zero errors.

LEO YUAN, PH.D.

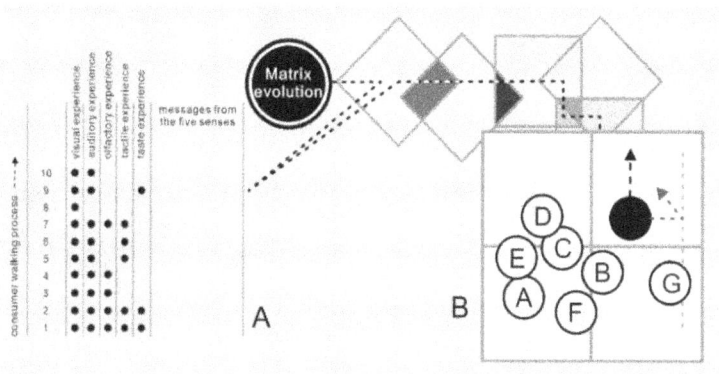

By Incorporating the Element of Time into the Matrix, The Entire Process Can Be Designed and Perfected

A: In terms of five-sense marketing planning, is there a design for each process from the outset that achieves sensory experiences and visions? What about hearing, smell, touch, and taste? By systematically evaluating each of these aspects, you can design an immersive sensory experience.

B: The matrix serves as a strategic thinking tool. When considering brand positioning from A to G, if a "black circle" brand moves to the right and cannot compete with the G brand, it may need to innovate upwards to create topicality and stand out.

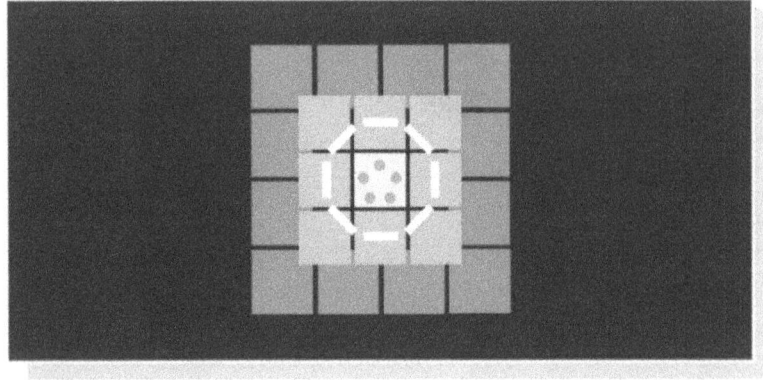

Nine-Box Grid Thinking, Mandala Thinking, Theoretical Overlay Thinking

From the five dots at the center (Five Elements), expand outward to the Eight Trigrams (Ba Gua), and then arrange into 9-Box Grid, covering the exterior with the Twelve Palaces. Can these four theories be integrated into one overarching theory or architecture?

By layering each smaller theory to construct a comprehensive theoretical framework, one might observe correlations between these theories and gain insight into the broader trends.

LEO YUAN, PH.D.

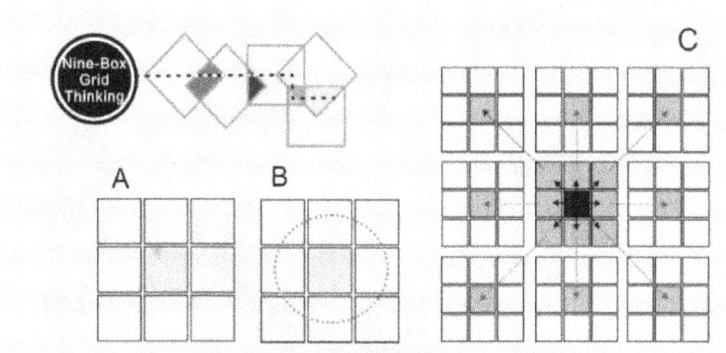

9-Box Grid's Spiral and Radial Thinking is User-Friendly and Comprehensive

A: Using the 9-Box Grid involves placing the topic in the central gray grid and filling the remaining eight boxes with ideas or solutions that come to mind.

B: 9-Box Grid Weekly Calendar: Write the key tasks for the upcoming week in the central gray grid. Each day, from Monday to Sunday, fill in the corresponding box with specific work details, focusing on the central tasks.

C: 9-Box Grid Network Expansion Method: The central black square represents you. Surrounding it are eight friends (dark gray), each of whom also connects to eight additional friends (light gray). This network quickly expands to include 64 new connections, facilitating business visits and opportunities.

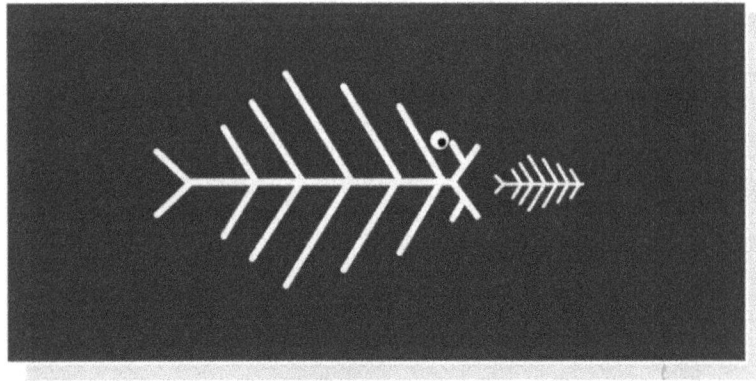

Fishbone Thinking Reflects How Nature Teaches Us to Understand the Unfolding of Problems

In nature, there are often objects we can observe and learn from, such as fish. Fishbone extend from the head to the tail and radiate from the center to both ends. Every detail is part of a larger system that can be categorized. Each element serves a specific function or role. By mapping out the fishbone structure of the entire system, one can clearly visualize the position and function of each process and component.

LEO YUAN, PH.D.

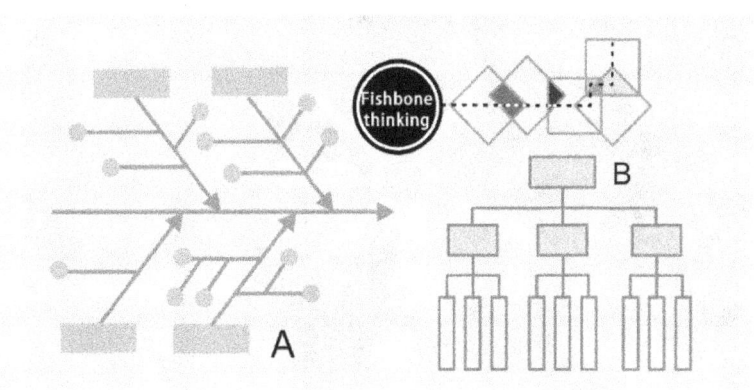

The Best Approach to Problem-Solving Involves Thoroughly Organizing All Relevant Contexts

A: The Fishbone diagram, also known as the Ishikawa diagram, was developed by Kaoru Ishikawa. It is a method used to identify the root causes of problems. This tool can be applied in planning activities, analyzing factory processes, and developing projects.

B: An organizational chart is commonly used to illustrate the structure and hierarchy within a company or department. This representation method can be extended to the Analytic Hierarchy Process (AHP), which is a method for systematically addressing complex problems. AHP provides hierarchical decomposition across different levels and facilitates quantitative evaluations to identify and comprehensively assess contexts.

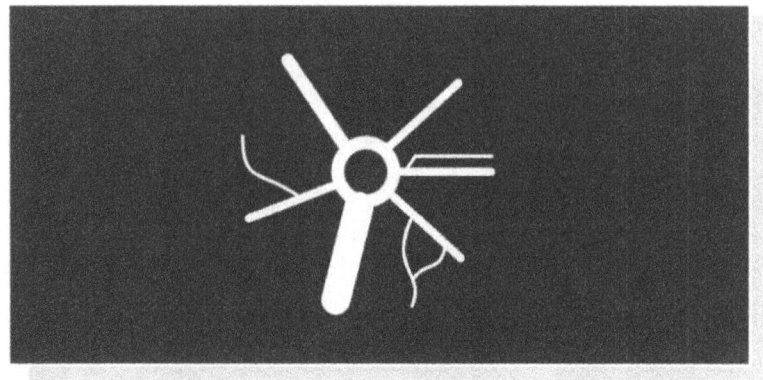

Map Association Refers to a Connection Map Jointly Created by Nature and Humans

Map thinking can also be linked to the development of theme branches on a map. The central circle represents the theme, which is further divided into five projects. Each project entails different operational details. Similarly, in thinking, one should initially grasp the theme and outline its structure. Subsequently collected data should be placed in appropriate locations based on this structure.

LEO YUAN, PH.D.

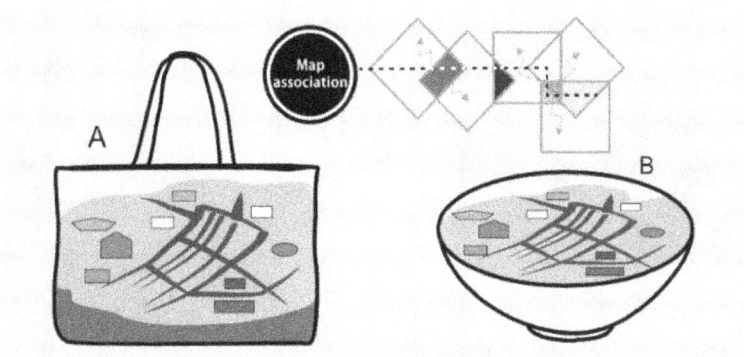

Maps Can Create Interactive Contact Diagrams or Be Directly Used to Produce Map Products

The simple concept of a map can be applied in various ways, even leading to the creation of new products.
A: Handbags can be adorned with printed maps, whether ancient or depicting a city. They can be paired with different outfits and also become fashion statements.
B: Town maps painted inside bowls turn them into unique town-themed products. Visitors can use the map and attraction signs inside the bowl to navigate or take it home as a souvenir to share with friends.

Letter Association Involves Combining Letters into Patterns Based on Their Sounds

Every language possesses unique letters, each akin to a simple picture that can be creatively arranged through clever combinations. Imagine letters as three-dimensional shapes: viewing them from different angles—up, down, left, and right—alters the scene completely. By creatively arranging letters, they can form unique patterns.

Letters are written symbols representing sounds. They can represent individual sounds or sequences of sounds. Letters and sounds inherently coexist.

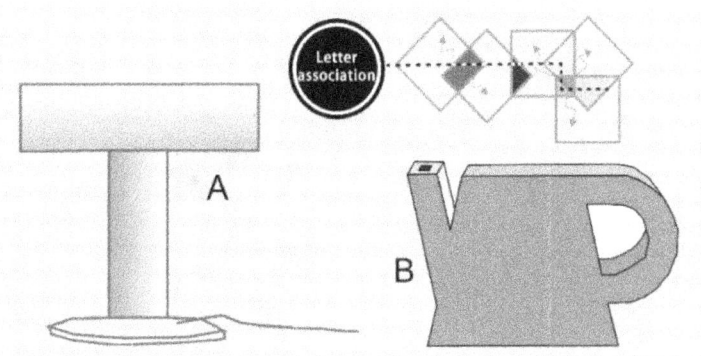

Thinking Beyond Letters as Mere Symbols Opens up Creative Possibilities

By using letters as a thematic anchor for association, any object can be connected to letter shapes. For example: A) The table lamp is designed in a T shape, and B) the teapot is associated with the letter P or other letters.

Text Units, even in Their Imperfection, Construct Complete Images in the Mind

When encountering words from various countries, even if their meaning is not understood, the absence of a single character can hinder comprehension. Each word resembles a simple and creative picture, revealing operational principles through their visual forms.

LEO YUAN, PH.D.

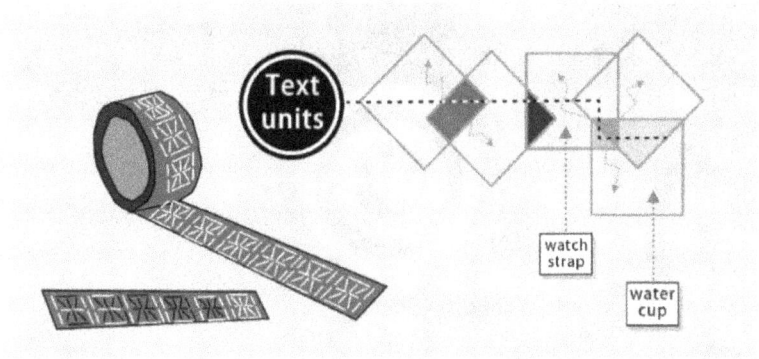

Using Textual Symbols in Product Design Offers Numerous Possibilities

Tape can be designed using textual units. If you need to write something, simply remove other lines. Similarly, watch straps can be designed with these textual units to personalize them with your name. They can also be used near water cups to easily label personal items like my own water glasses.

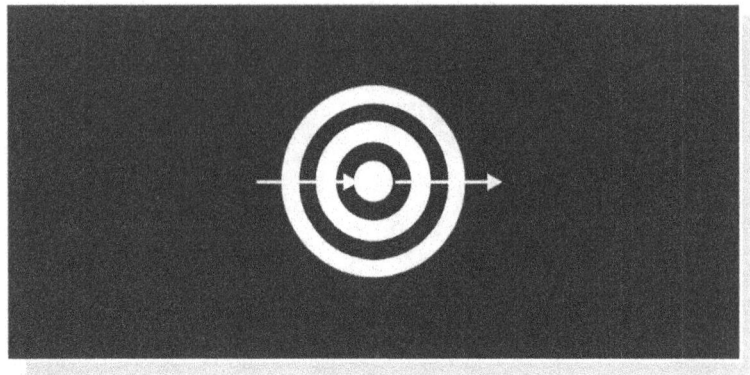

If You Grasp the Key Points, You Will Achieve Twice the Results with Half the Effort and Reach Your Target Easily

Everything has at least one key point, which is the most important factor that defines the unique function or feature of that thing. Sometimes the key point is obvious, sometimes it is not visible, and it is often taken for granted and ignored.

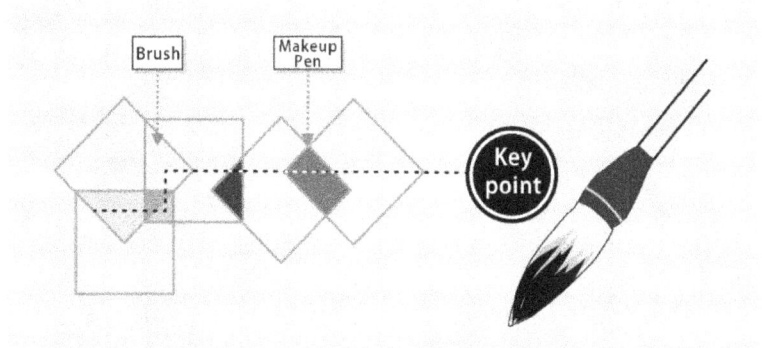

The Transfer of a Key Technology Can Save a Company

When everyone sees a brush, what they care about is what kind of hair this brush is made of. However, the key focus of the brush lies in the selection and processing of wool materials, as well as the technology used to bind these materials together. This key technology can also be applied to cosmetic pens and brushes to create more durable products made from wool.

A film company produces high-end skin care products because it possesses the following technologies: 1. Crystal micro-technology for micronizing ingredients, 2. Collagen technology, which is the main raw material of the film, and 3. Antioxidant technology to prevent oxidation. These film manufacturing technologies can be applied to cosmetics and skin care products.

When Examining the Structure of Things, There Should Be a Key Focus

The key focus and key technology can become a theme and be extrapolated to other fields. Because it is a key technology here, it may also play a crucial role in other fields and potentially become an innovative product in those fields.

LEO YUAN, PH.D.

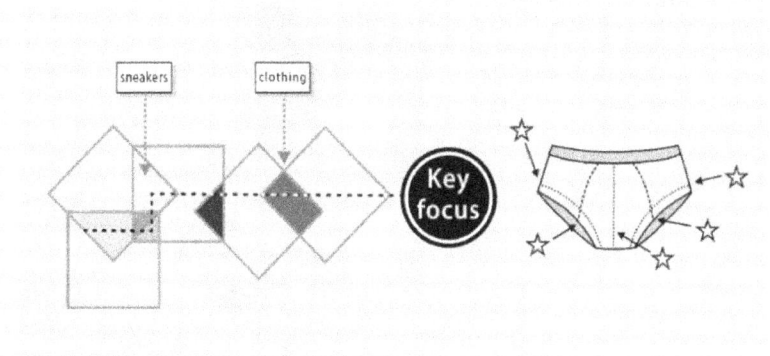

The Secret to Making a Product Easy to Use Lies in Reinforcing Its Key Focus

What are the key elements of men's underwear? The answer is the thread. If the thread is of good quality and strong, the underwear will not easily break. However, if the manufacturer buys low-quality, easily breakable threads to save costs, consumers will frequently complain that the underwear falls apart after only a few wears. What if these key considerations are applied to clothing and sneakers? It should be possible to identify the crucial factors that enhance product durability.

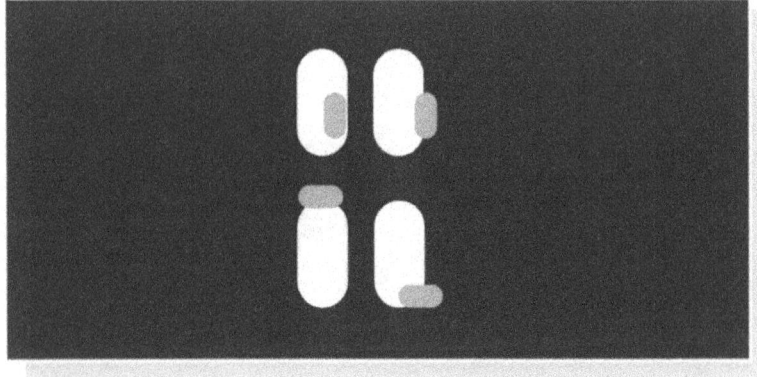

Parent-Child Relationships Are Akin to Symbiosis in Nature

Many symbiotic relationships exist in nature. For instance, elephants often host egrets standing on their bodies, as egrets feed on parasites hidden in the elephant's skin folds. Without them, these blood-sucking insects would bite the elephant, causing discomfort and itching. It appears that small animals depend on larger ones, but in reality, larger animals also rely on smaller ones. We can similarly apply this concept of mutual dependency in our own lives.

LEO YUAN, PH.D.

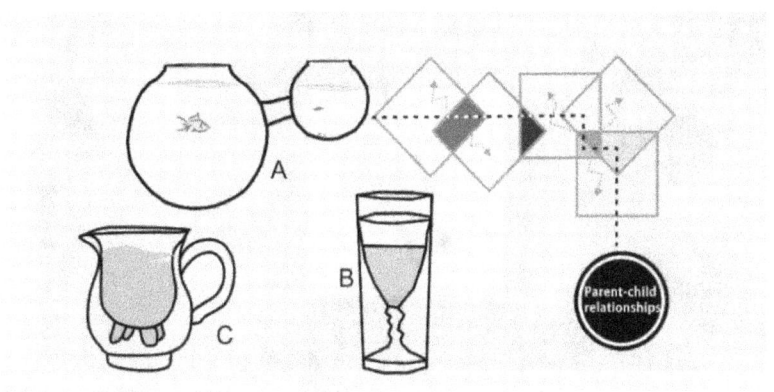

Big Fish and Small Fish, Big Cups and Small Cups, Arranged in Pairs to Create New Shapes

When arranging a parent-to-child setup, consider the size and design of the interior and exterior configurations:

A: Have large fish tanks and small fish tanks. This allows the big fish space to hunt while providing the small fish room to escape and hide.

B: Place an elegant wine glass inside an ordinary cup, or place a cow-shaped cup inside a glass(C).

Two-in-One Arrangement Allows for Perfect Integration and Mutual Support

It involves merging two different individuals into one, or combining two identical objects into one, or adding a new function to an existing object. In market practice, this can also apply to integrating two departments. When one department adds new business, the department that is relieved of that responsibility can focus solely on its core activities.

LEO YUAN, PH.D.

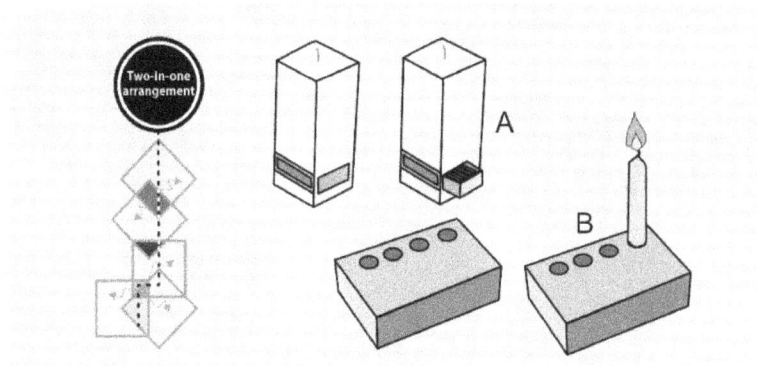

By Combining Different Elements with Consistent Behavioral Goals, You Can Develop Useful Products

A: Create a hole at the bottom of the candle and insert a box of matches directly into it.
B: Drill four round holes in the matchbox to insert candles.
This kind of thinking also embodies the concept of self-service. It involves combining accessories needed for an object. For instance, matches are essential for lighting a candle, and the candle requires an upright mold, so the matchbox's three-dimensional shape is utilized.

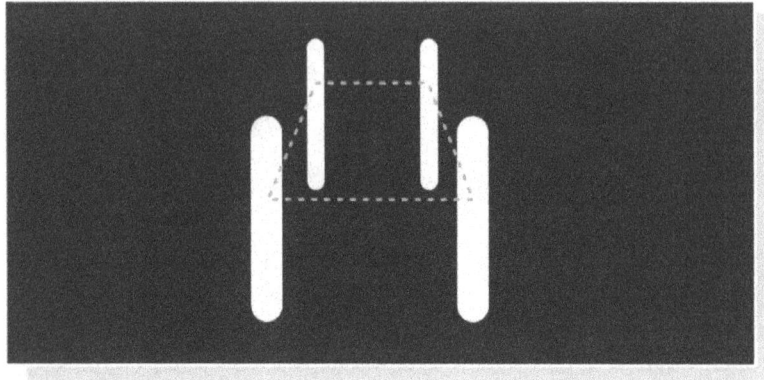

Tubular Arrangement Involves the Use of Tubular Design in Various Applications

Tubular thinking acknowledges the numerous tubes present in our lives, many of which are buried underground such as water pipes. These pipes facilitate numerous daily tasks, including waste management and providing clean water. Their organized and systematic arrangement ensures they can efficiently fulfill their purpose. It's worth considering the application of this tubular system, often overlooked despite its ubiquitous presence.

LEO YUAN, PH.D.

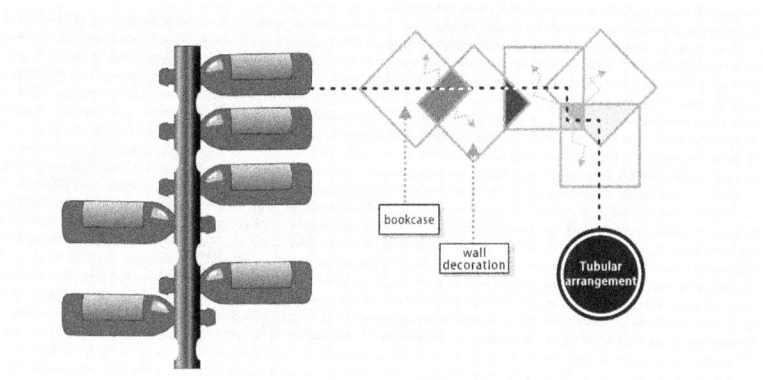

Water Pipe and Wine Cabinet: A Creative Combination of Two Unrelated Items

Drill holes in water pipes and use them as bottle racks.

This tubular wine cabinet appears to be an innovative design, but creative thinking is actually a simple technique. Similar to "Trigger Concepts", where I randomly selected an object—in this case, the "water pipe"—and began to ponder how it could be used as a wine cabinet. Similarly, could water pipes be utilized as bookcases or wall decorations?

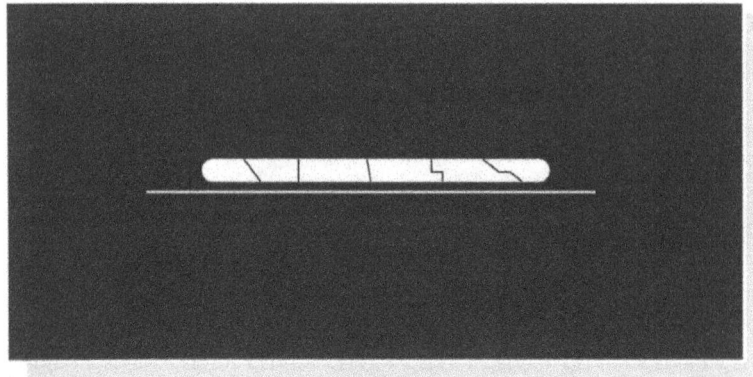

Planar Thinking Involves Pressing All Three-Dimensional Objects into a Plane

Thinking in planes, three-dimensional pipelines can also be designed for flat transmission, and the organization of stacked houses can be considered in flat management. The biggest advantage of flat-screen TVs is that they free up living space and make the living room appear larger.

Planar thinking can help us approach problems from a different perspective. While we may not always achieve the goal of thinking purely in planes, we may generate good ideas during the process.

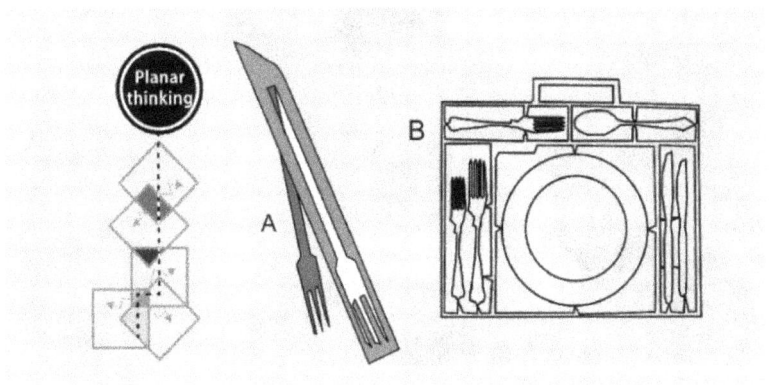

Flat Products Do Not Occupy Space and Are Sometimes More Convenient

A: A flat plate cut into the shape of a fork allows all similar tableware to be laid flat in a suitcase without taking up space.

B: All the cutlery—plates, forks, knives, and spoons—are cut from a single flat plate, fitting the size of a handbag for easy carrying.

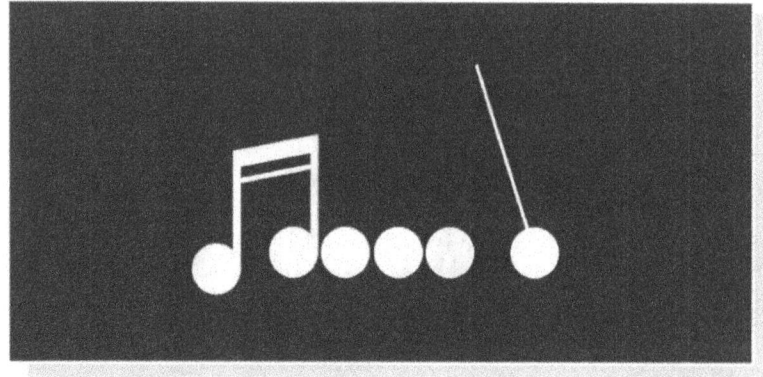

Musical Arrangements Involve Attempting to Use Music to Make Things Function

You can compose new music, create new instruments, explore new sounds, and develop new musical activities. But can you link music with a ball? A music ball. Or imagine raising chickens with music? Musical chicken raising.
1. Integrate music into everything as a medium.
2. Use music to replace traditional signals or combine it with signals to convey specific messages or instructions.
3. Utilize the psychological or physiological effects of music to benefit humanity.
4. Transform noise into musical sounds.

LEO YUAN, PH.D.

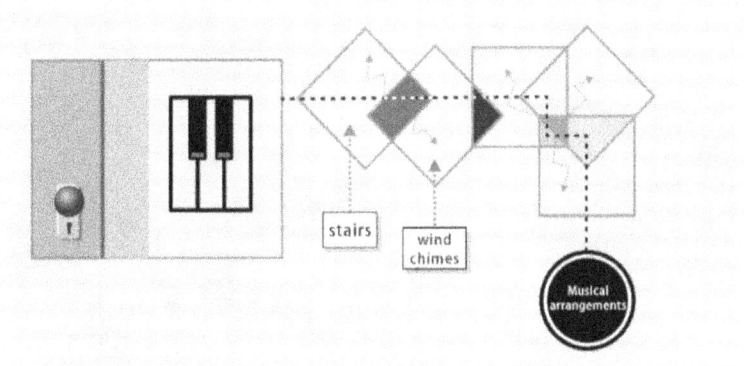

Music Serves as the Doorbell, with Close Acquaintances Using Intimate Musical Passwords

The piano keyboard-shaped music doorbell has five tones: Do, #Do, Re, #Re, Mi. Visitors listen to the agreed-upon music upon arrival. It can also function as a key to unlock the door: set a sequence of music and press the corresponding keys to open the door directly.

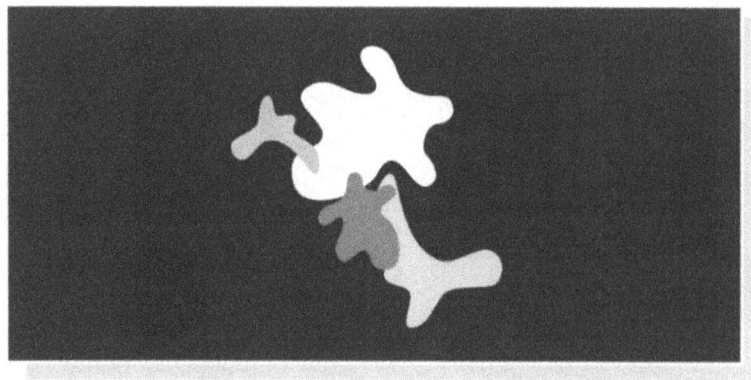

Variable Association Means the Shape is not Fixed but Can Be Customized at Will

The greatest advantage of variable association is that it liberates your thinking from traditional constraints.

Use the Amoeba desk for flexible assembly based on different meeting or project needs. In an Amoeba organization, personnel can be reassigned as needed for projects, fostering multi-functional employees capable of supporting departments facing tight manpower constraints at any time.

LEO YUAN, PH.D.

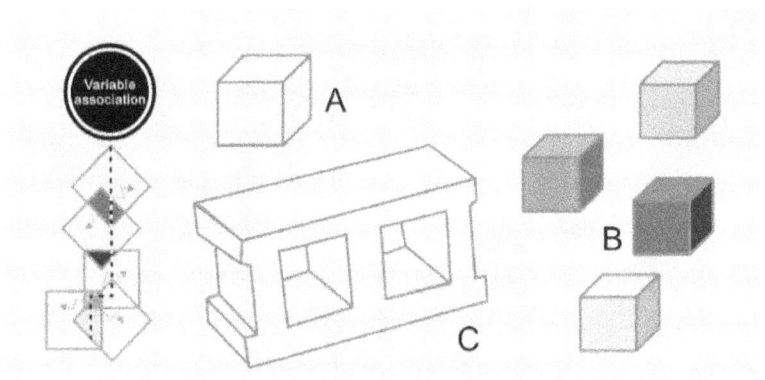

Powdered Sugar Can Be Molded into the Shape of a Sugar Cube and Can Also Be "Deformed" into Other Shapes

A: Sugar cube. Open a mold and shape the powdered sugar into a cube. This is the well-known sugar cube.

B: Use a mold resembling a sugar cube and fill it with different contents to create various types of cube shapes, such as Chinese medicine cubes, grain cubes, and colored sugar cubes.

C: Alternatively, use a different mold to create uniquely shaped sugar cubes. You can even stack them like building blocks and use your creativity to form various shapes.

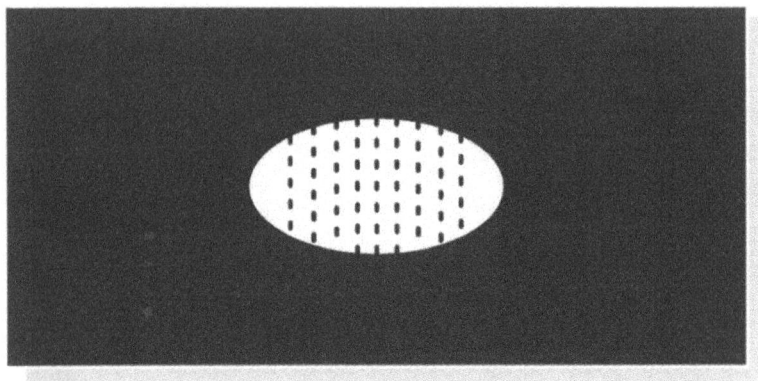

Associating with Clouds, Every Item Appears Soft and Gentle

Think of clouds. The clouds that accompany us every day appear different each day. They float so high that they cannot be touched, yet they appear soft. At times, they appear heavy, releasing rain heavily. Their ever-changing nature has made clouds a topic in numerous novels and fairy tales.

If you carefully analyze a cloud, you will discover it actually serves many physical functions. Each operational principle could inspire a corresponding creative product.

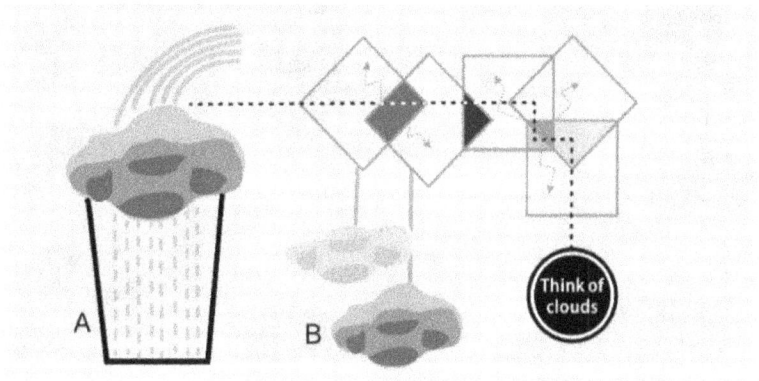

Cloud-Locking Begins the Process of Deducing Changes to Any Product

A: Create a cloud-shaped ceramic with numerous small holes drilled in the center. Place it over a water glass and pour water through; it will simulate rain.

B: Crafting cloud-shaped chandeliers sparks unlimited imagination for children and may provide soothing effects for individuals frequently in a bad mood.

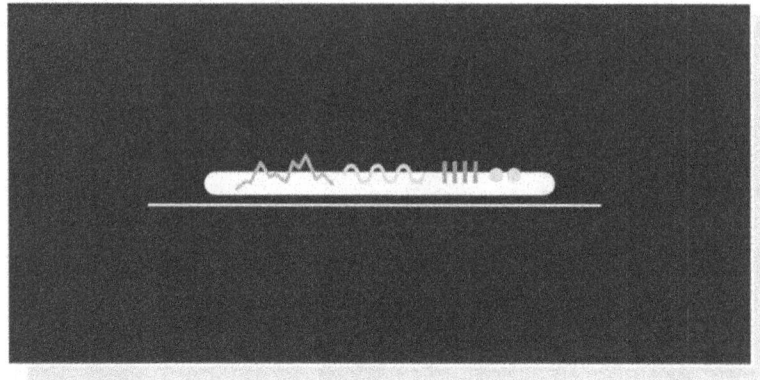

Natural Associations, Connections with Natural Elements, Are Simply Endless

Natural association involves imitation in creation, a method of inventing and crafting by mimicking the shapes of various natural objects. Shapes inspired by nature have spurred human creativity, influencing creations such as hieroglyphs, boxing movements, dance postures, cutlery, armor, and architectural designs.

1. Same object but different shapes: One object takes on multiple forms, such as animal-shaped biscuits and sunflower-shaped biscuits.

2. Different objects with the same shape: Multiple objects share a single shape, like an elephant-shaped pencil box and an elephant-shaped table lamp.

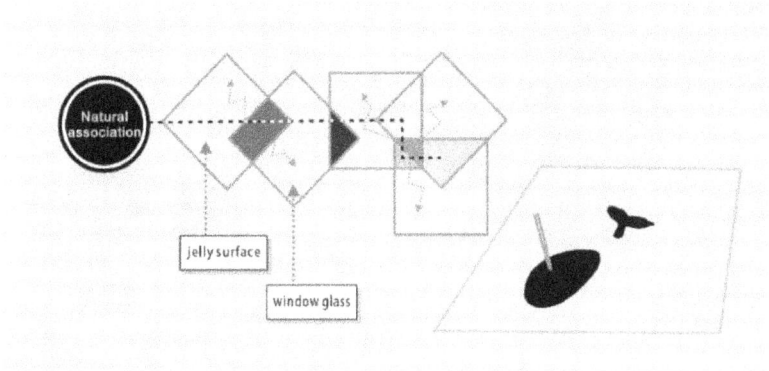

If the Desktop Were an Ocean and Jelly Was the Earth...

Imagine the desktop as the sea, and design a pen holder shaped like a whale. Similarly, consider jelly as a landmass with mountains and water. The jelly can have an uneven surface; when you pour creamer on it, it resembles mountain topography. By designing raised text, you can create messages like 'happy birthday'. When the birthday celebrant pours creamer, they'll be pleasantly surprised.

Consider if it were window glass—could you achieve a similar effect?

Animal Association Reveals the Myriad Structural Designs Animals Employ for Survival

Bionics, a science that mimics the unique abilities of living organisms, innovates new machinery and technologies by studying their structural and functional principles.

Woodpeckers peck tree trunks daily with their long beaks at speeds of 7 meters per second, up to 15-20 times per second, yet experience no concussive damage due to the woodpecker's head being designed to absorb and buffer shock. Safety helmets worn by construction workers or military personnel mimic the woodpecker's head structure to achieve optimal shock absorption.

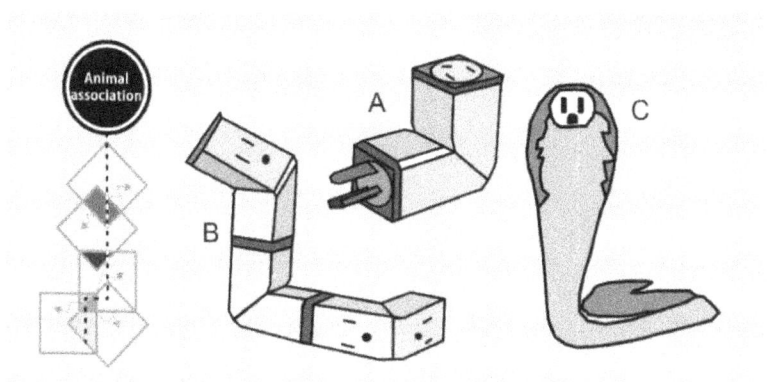

Simply Pick Any Snake at Random and You Can Make Creative Associations

A: Design sockets and plugs with angled surfaces that can be rotated.
B: By extending this design, sockets and plugs can be expanded infinitely.
C: Create a cobra directly, with its head serving as the socket.
Any animal can inspire creative product designs, including snakes. For instance, the skin could store discs individually. Alternatively, you could embellish a transmission line with a beautiful snake design. By merging the function of the object with the appearance of the animal, a wide range of creative animal-themed products can be developed.

www.ingramcontent.com/pod-product-compliance
Lightning Source LLC
Chambersburg PA
CBHW060151050426
42446CB00013B/2775